Endorser

Impressions of Near-Death Experiences contains powerful and transformative testimonies from people of different religious and cultural backgrounds who experienced NDEs and their aftereffects. Profoundly insightful, your perspective on Heaven and the afterlife will be life changing. A must read.

ANITA MOORJANI
New York Times best-selling author of *Dying to Be Me*, *What If This Is Heaven*, and *Sensitive Is the New Strong.*

This important book is about the wonderful, impressive, and universal stories shared by people who had a near-death experience (NDE). By reading about the different elements of an NDE you will be surprised by how these experiences will change your current worldview, and what we may learn is that it is all about love and compassion toward yourself and others, and that everything and everybody is always connected. You are not your body, but you are pure consciousness that sometimes can be experienced during a period of a non-functioning brain. This wonderful book has the potential to break many taboos about our current ideas about life and death, and we can reap the benefits of the NDE without having to nearly die. Highly recommended!

PIM VAN LOMMEL
Cardiologist, NDE-researcher, author of *Consciousness Beyond Life*

Selected quotes from the actual reports of over one hundred near-death experience accounts, thoughtfully categorized under a broad spectrum of major headings by an investigator with decades of rigorous experience studying the entire field, make this book a treasure trove of information for those seeking deeper understanding of this fascinating aspect of human experience. A most worthwhile read!

EBEN ALEXANDER, MD
Former Harvard Neurosurgeon and author of *Proof of Heaven*, *The Map of Heaven*, and *Living in a Mindful Universe.*

Impressions of Near-Death Experiences

Quotations From Over
100 Experiencers

Robert Christophor Coppes, PhD

IANDS Publications

International Association for
Near-Death Studies, Durham, NC

International Association for Near-Death Studies (IANDS)
2741 Campus Walk Avenue, Building 500
Durham, North Carolina 27705-8878
www.iands.org

ISBN-13: 978-0-9975608-9-3

Cover design by Robert Christophor Coppes.
Cover photo of painting by Claude Monet
Impression, Soleil Levant (*Impression, Sunrise*),
courtesy of Musée Marmottan Monet, Paris.
Unless otherwise noted, photos are courtesy of the subject.

Table of Contents

Preface

The front cover of this book depicts part of the painting *Impression, Soleil Levant (Impression, Sunrise)* by Claude Monet. When the painting was shown together with other paintings in an exhibition in Paris in 1874, the reviews were mixed. Some were favorable—that is, modern and forward thinking; others were downright negative—that is, traditional. In a satirical review following that one painting by Monet, artists of his genre were scornfully called "Impressionists" because their paintings were considered unfinished and merely an impression or sketch of what the final painting should have been. This critique gave the art movement its name: Impressionism. Since that time, the world has come to greatly appreciate Impressionists—just look at the sky-high prices for their paintings—because we realize that we don't need a fully elaborated, realistic picture to have a fair impression of what is depicted or what is the core message of the painting. In fact, the "impression" can actually evoke more feeling and meaning than a mere realistic copy would have.

Similarly, my purpose in this book is to give an impression of what near-death experiences (NDEs) are like by giving a multitude of quotes from more than 100 experiencers (NDErs) from all over the world. They originate from North and South America, Europe, and the Middle and Far East, including China. There are even quotes from as far away as New Zealand. The original religious beliefs of the NDErs in this book are equally diverse, representing Hinduism, Judaism, Buddhism, Christianity, and Islam, as well as atheism.

An impression is all I can offer because, in the end—or the near-end, in this case—no one knows exactly how it all really works. After all, when it comes to NDEs, what we are talking about is of a totally different order, a totally different dimension. So, my advice is that if someone tells you that they know exactly what the afterlife is about, you should run quickly away. An impression is actually all that is possible.

To appreciate the contents of this book, I suggest that, similar to appreciating an Impressionist painting, you read the quotes and sense how they affect you. Feel what they tell you—but *really* feel. Put your 'traditional' ideas aside. Let go of whatever ways you have been programmed by your upbringing or from religion, and open your mind to receive whatever wisdom you find in these testimonies of people who have experienced the first moments of physical death. I believe that their messages will touch a truth that is deep within you—an inner core that you can trust.

A note on reading this book. Whenever an experiencer's name is known—either their actual name or possibly a pseudonym they have given themself or another author has given them—it appears in their story below. If a story does not include a name, it is because it comes from an anonymous source such as the repository of NDEs of the International Association for Near-Death Studies or the Near-Death Experience Research Foundation.

Acknowledgments

Although I enjoyed creating this impressionist painting of NDEs, I must say it was an ambitious project. I wouldn't have been able to do it without the help and good will of so many others.

First of all, I would like to thank both the International Association for Near-Death Studies (IANDS; www.iands .org) and the Near-Death Experience Research Foundation (NDERF; www.nderf.org) for their extensive archives of NDE narratives from which I drew much of the material for this book. Both of their websites are available online to the public. Their archives and other online materials make both organizations unique, and they offer a vital service to humanity, for which I am very grateful. Another wonderful organization that provides online materials is the Belgian www .Ponto3.org.

Then there are the NDErs that I had the privilege to speak with and to interview, as well as the NDErs who had painstakingly written their experiences in the books that I read. I realize that I was able to draw from only a small selection of the many amazing books that are available.

I would like to thank the following people:

- Jan Holden for her unwavering support and valuable editing, and Robert and Suzanne Mays for their final editing,
- Robert Mays, Anneliese Fox, and Alinaghi Ghasemiannejad (IANDS), Jody Long (NDERF), and Noël

Acknowledgments

van Herreweghe (Ponto3) for bringing me into contact with many NDErs,

- Marjorie Woollacott, Natalie Bonthius, and Debbie James (IANDS), Mally Cox-Chapman, Liz Dale, Djamil Graham, Robert and Suzanne Mays, Maurice Oosterhof, Titus Rivas, and Rudolf Smit for their support,
- Nancy Evans Bush for her invaluable comments and input when I was writing Chapter 8 on distressing NDEs, and for her down-to-earth, cheerful views, both solicited and unsolicited,
- Chris Carson, Rachel Finch, and Lee Thornton Riggs for pre-reading the manuscript,
- the following NDErs for their outright enthusiastic response to my project: Kimberlee Anderson, Jane Bannister, Irina Berghout, Anna Best, Silvia Bulten-Bolk, Brigitte Buyle, Chris Carson, Christina, Anoeska Coopman, Ellyn Dye, Rachel Finch, Bill and Gayle Gladstone, Jang Jaswal, Brooke Jones, Rene Jorgensen, Tienke Klein, Geertrui Lagae, Mirjam Leféber, Deirdre DeWitt Maltby, Kathy McDaniel, Andrew Petro, Tetty Pols-Visser, Marijke Redant, Catja de Rijk, Nancy Rynes, Kimberly Clark Sharp, Yvonne Sneeden, Yazmine Star, Yolaine Stout, Azmina Suleman, Scott Taylor, Lee Thornton Riggs, Rosemary Thornton, Vu Tran, Carol Lynn Vengroff, Johan Verhage, and Noël de Waele.
- Rosemary Mitchell-Schuitevoerder for checking the English in my first version.

CHAPTER 1

Out of the Body

An NDE can happen to anyone: young or old, rich or poor, male or female. And the circumstances under which an NDE takes place are very diverse. Many cases happen in a medically critical situation such as during cardiac arrest or after an accident. But other NDEs have occurred during an existential or psychological crisis. There are stories of people who had their NDEs during deep meditation or prayer. And there are even examples in which an NDE seems to have occurred for no reason at all; for an example, see Rene Jorgensen's case below. In this sense, the term "NDE" is misleading, as it gives the impression that it can occur only when one is near death. Because research has revealed that, under seemingly identical physical circumstances, most people remember nothing unusual whereas a relatively small minority recall an NDE, it is still unclear what exactly causes the experience. Considering just the extreme situation of cardiac arrest, only a minority who has survived it has reported an NDE. Why is that?

There are several possible answers. Assuming that during an NDE a person's spirit has left their body, the cardiac arrest could have been too short, allowing too little time for the disconnection to occur. However, researchers have found no relationship between length of medical crisis and presence or absence of an NDE. It is also possible that not everyone remembers their NDE—that the experience remains hidden in the NDEr's unconscious mind. A good example of this

1

situation is the case of Stephanie Arnold. Her 2015 book about it, *37 Seconds*, reads like an exciting novel.

Her story begins with a very strong premonition that she would die during the imminent birth of her child. Other people ascribed her panic to fear of childbirth.

When she finally went into labor, things went horribly wrong. After the delivery, which took place by Caesarean section, the placenta was removed, resulting in a near-fatal and very rare amniotic fluid embolism. Her heart stopped but was restarted after 37 seconds with firm chest compressions by one of the nurses.

After her condition was stabilized, she was kept in a medically induced coma for another week. Then she recovered and started looking for answers. She wanted to know how her strong premonition had come true.

With regression therapy, she went back to the moment of childbirth and found herself separated from her body. She was standing next to her body in the operating room, watching everything that went on. Later, she was able to describe the entire procedure correctly, with the exact locations of staff members in the operating room. She later recognized the nurse who had cracked her ribs while starting her heart with chest compressions. She also felt herself floating through the corridors of the hospital, seeing things that later were confirmed.

Eventually, she shot into the air and ended up in a bright white area where she met deceased relatives, including her father-in-law. He showed her a foreign coin. After the regression therapy, she asked her family about the meaning of the coin. For her brother-in-law, this coin in the hands of his late father turned out to have a significant meaning.

So, it had been a real NDE, with clear evidence, but it had been hidden until she relived it through regression.

An NDE can begin in various ways. Some people perceive their "soul," "spirit," "essence," or "consciousness" leaving their physical body; others don't. Once out-of-body, some experiencers find themselves perceiving the material world. They may float above their body, or they may stand looking at it. Sometimes they don't realize they've left their body, and sometimes they don't even realize that the body lying there is theirs. That may sound crazy, but it is not that strange when we consider that we know our own mirror reflection well, but when outside the body, we see ourselves in 3D and from a different angle—one from which we apparently don't always recognize ourselves.

Some people then unexpectedly find themselves in a cave, tunnel, or other kind of passage and then suddenly arrive in an entirely different, unearthly place. Some people skip the passage altogether but end up in that unearthly environment in a completely different way. There they may see beautiful, unearthly colors; hear unearthly music; and meet deceased loved ones and other spiritual entities.

The examples in this chapter show that leaving the body and existing outside of it is a very special—and often confusing—experience.

──────── EXITING THE BODY IS EASY ────────

At the moment of my death, I popped out of my body like toast out of a toaster. (Thornton, 2021, p. 3)

From One Room to Another
Juliet Nightingale had two NDEs and several other spiritually transformative experiences—a term coined by Canadian psychiatrist Yvonne Kason. Juliet had her first NDE when she was terminally ill with colon cancer. It was in the mid-1970s just prior to when psychiatrist Raymond Moody coined the term "NDE." She wrote that transitioning to the other world is very easy. On her website, which is still up and running, she wrote:

The best way I can describe the transition from being "alive" on the physical plane and the passage to the Other Side is like passing from one "room" to another. You do not cease to be or lose consciousness; your consciousness simply shifts from one vantage point to another. The experience changes; your outlook changes; your feelings change. And the feelings I experienced were profound. For me, it most certainly became that peace that surpasses all understanding. . . . (Nightingale, 2006–2009)

For years, Juliet had a radio program, and in 2009 she transitioned finally to that other world.

Top of My Head

As a young woman, Jane Bannister almost lost her life due to anorexia. She tells how she left her body:

I had starved myself. Like all anorexics, I had no idea that I was ill, and had run around for weeks fueled by nervous energy rather than physical energy . . . I found myself exiting my body by floating through the top of my head. It was like being born, but entering another world through the head. A powerful male being with a cloak and helmet was behind me, arms outstretched. From his fingers came a magnetic force which was pulling me out of my body. I saw my lifeless body lying on the bed. I started screaming mentally, "I don't want to die. I'm only eighteen!" . . . Incidentally, years later when the film "Star Wars" came out, I saw a cinema poster and almost fainted in the street because I recognized Darth Vader as the evil figure who had pulled me out of my body . . . Two years later I had another NDE when I accidentally committed suicide by taking an overdose as the

4

result of a broken love affair. This time it was a much more pleasant experience. I was gently removed from my body by an angel. (Anonymous, 2010, December 20, 16:40)

Pulled From My Body

In his amazing book, *Awaking After Life*, Rene Jorgensen wrote how he was sitting on a beach in India with a girl from Japan when he suddenly left his body. He had a very complete NDE without having been in a critical medical situation:

> A power from within me revealed itself and fought the old part in me. For the first time, my ego was fighting to stay alive in an endless uncharted ocean . . . I was suddenly no longer observing what was happening from inside my body. I found myself outside my body in the air above where we were sitting . . . The sensation of being pulled from my body was overwhelmingly powerful. I felt a deep explosion, like a volcanic eruption, pull my body apart and dissolve the essence of what I once knew as myself. I was suddenly naked, exposed to everything in the entire universe, but at the same time I was bathed in the transparent light of something so powerful, so indescribable, all words fade and disappear. (Jorgensen, 2007, pp. 4–6)

Power Drained From My Body

In her book, *It Can Happen to All of Us*, Catja de Rijk wrote about her NDE that started during cardiac catheterization. She was not afraid of the operation, and she had even been very cheerful. She was able to follow the operation on a monitor, and everything seemed to be going well. Suddenly she felt an excruciating pain in her chest unlike any she had experienced before. At the same time, several alarms went off in the operating room, and there was panic among the doctors and nurses around her.

> I also noticed that the strength was draining from my legs. It started in my toes, and it crawled up until I completely lost feeling in my legs. Immediately afterwards, the power started to drain from my fingers and hands, from my arms and also from my upper body. The pain in my chest disappeared and an unbelievably beautiful calm came over me. I was not in a panic, and I felt a total surrender and peace. (De Rijk, 2021, p. 30)

I Am Not My Body

Sometimes leaving the body is "a piece of cake"—effortless, as in the case of Ellyn Dye. Her NDE can be found on her website, and she described it in a very fun and entertaining way.

It was dusk when she was driving her car, about to enter an intersection with a green light. Another car was about to enter the intersection from the other direction. Then suddenly the driver turned into her lane. A collision could not be avoided.

> But suddenly, with no effort on my part, I was literally out of my body! I was actually excited about that! I looked down and saw the two cars crunched into each other, and I saw the man from the other car get out and walk over to my car. I thought he was walking over to see if I was all right. He reached in through the open window on the driver's side, and he turned my headlights off. I thought that was strange, but I lost interest in what was going on.

Later, in the hospital, a police officer would hand her a traffic ticket for driving without headlights.

As she floated outside her body above the crunched cars, she wondered who "I" is:

> Being out of my body was an amazing experience! I suddenly realized that if "I" was hovering above my car, while my body was inside the car, unconscious, then my whole idea and belief of who "I" was, was totally wrong! As most people in our material society do, I had identified my "self" with my body. I believed that "I" was my body, that my body was, in fact, who I am—all of who I am. But suddenly, I knew without a doubt that was wrong. "I"—my consciousness, the part of me that can think and feel—was no longer in my body, so it seemed obvious that my body is something that "I" occupy, rather than being what "I" am! And as I really came to terms with that concept, I realized that "I" was so much more than I had ever imagined. Being out of my body felt like I had been released from tight restraints that I had worn for a very long time. I felt totally free for the first time in my life . . . Without a body, I could "see" in every direction simultaneously, even without physical eyes to see. The sudden loss of my body was not a hardship; being IN my body had been the hardship, and now I was FREE! (Dye, 2023)

CONFUSING: IS THAT ME?

Dual Perspective

While driving, an Iranian man who calls himself Arshan, didn't feel well when he reached an intersection. Even though he said he looked both ways, he was nevertheless hit by a car he hadn't seen coming. The next moment he was hovering above the intersection where he saw a body on the ground. After some time, he recognized himself. By that time, people had gathered to help him. He knew they were talking, but he couldn't hear what they said. There was something else, instead:

> When I looked at these people, I knew their thoughts and what they were going to say.

An ambulance was rushed to the scene, and Arshan was taken to the hospital. He saw that the medics were trying to save his life. He saw everything from above, from just below the ceiling of the operating room. He noticed that he was both detached from his body but also still inside his body. This dual feeling is reported by some other NDErs as well.

In his account, Arshan tried to describe what it was like to be outside his body. He said that he was in a non-physical form that was like a human form. But it was very different and very nice. He felt wonderful. He mentioned that sight was the only sense he had, and he could see more than he had been able to see in his physical body.

> I felt like I had turned into energy. (*Arshan NDE*, 1996)

Phone Booth

A woman's infection began with a sore throat and a high fever. At one point she was hospitalized. Her doctor visited her twice a day, and during one of these visits, things went wrong.

> But one morning, it was different. I had this incredible and overwhelming sadness. I could only move my head at this point. He stayed, and he asked me to focus on his words . . . it was taking too much energy to listen. I could hear his voice, but then the words weren't clear.

I relaxed, and all of a sudden, I was on the ceiling. It was smooth and so quick. Now I could hear his words clearly and understand what his story was about.

Now I'm looking down at the woman lying in the bed, and I think, "Oh, I used to have a nightgown just like that one." Then I figured it out, "If I'm up here, and she is down there; this can't be good."

Her spirit then had the chance to briefly wander around in the hospital.

I found myself inside a phone booth that was built into the hallway wall. My husband was on the phone with my best friend. He was telling her what was happening. When she would respond, I would be in her office in North Carolina. When he would speak, I would be back in the phone booth. This went on for a while, and I was able to notice changes that my friend had made in her office decor. (Anonymous, 2019, October 17)

I Am Only Thoughts

One day, a 22-year-old teacher was bicycling home from her work at a primary school. A car came out of a side street and should have stopped for her, but she was hit and fell on the back of her head. She didn't want to lie on the ground within sight of her students. With much difficulty she got up—but fell again.

After that, it all became very confusing for her. She remembered that it was completely dark and that she heard an ambulance siren wailing. How she got into the ambulance, she did not know. The next moment she remembered was in the hospital. That is where her NDE started.

From a slightly higher vantage point, she saw a lot of activity of hospital staff around a body. She did not realize at all that the body lying there on the table surrounded by the doctors and nurses was hers.

Where am I? What happened?

She felt herself floating, without a body. That was very strange. She established that she couldn't see herself but that she was still thinking. She clearly was somewhere, she obviously had something left of her, but they were only thoughts. She said:

> But I was still thinking, and my emotions were also there, which meant I must be somewhere.

The activity around that body below her continued, but she turned around and proceeded into the dark, naturally, almost automatically. (Coppes, 2020, p. 143)

Lightning Struck Her Umbrella

As described in her amazing book *Changed in a Flash*, Elizabeth Krohn was in her car in the parking lot of a Houston, Texas, synagogue. Virtually out of nowhere a heavy thunderstorm suddenly arose. She had planned to go with her two boys to a remembrance service. She took her umbrella and got out of her car. After walking a few steps, lightning struck her umbrella. Although she heard a deafening bang and had a prickly sensation, she felt no pain at all, so she hurried on into the synagogue.

Her children had already arrived in the entrance hall, but they were crying their eyes out and were terribly confused. There was huge consternation in the congregation, and she did not quite understand why—nor could she understand why people paid attention only to her children and not to her. Suddenly she realized that she didn't have her umbrella with her anymore. She turned around, and through the synagogue window she saw her blackened umbrella in the parking lot. A little further she saw her body lying on the ground. Slowly it dawned on her that she was dead.

Soon after, she saw a glow of light that invited her to come along, which she did. Her extensive NDE, she said, lasted for two weeks, while in earthly terms she regained her consciousness after only a few minutes (Krohn & Kripal, 2018, pp. 16–19).

No Connection to That Body

This NDE account is from Bill Gladstone, my literary agent in the US. His NDE has not been published anywhere, but he offered to share it with me for this project.

> I was 15 years old and went to see my family physician for a flu shot. This was in 1966, and in those days even young children were given flu shots. He gave me the shot and told me that he would return in two minutes—that I should just sit on the chair in the examining room where he had given me the shot. I felt a little lightheaded but otherwise I felt fine. Suddenly I was no longer in my body.
>
> My next memory is being in a state of bliss in the corner of the examining room next to the ceiling. I looked down and saw a man in a white coat making loud noises. I paid further attention and made the connection that the man in the white coat was a medical doctor. I could sense that he was distraught and then observed that he was trying to revive a body that was on the floor. I had the realization that the body on the floor was mine. I did not feel connected to the body and did not recognize the doctor as my family physician even though I would so normally, as I had known him for many years. I was not

at all alarmed but did not want him to be worried and realized that the doctor's concern was the lifeless body on the floor that would not respond to him.

Bill then encountered loving beings, connected with them, felt an enormous amount of love, and became aware of important eternal wisdom (see the relevant chapters that follow). Then, in order to stop the doctor from suffering any longer, he decided to re-enter his body.

FLOATING AWAY

I Had Forgotten

Lee Thornton wrote an impressive book about her life: *Through Heaven's Gate and Back*. It is impressive not only because of her NDE but also because it is about ultimately coming to terms with her father's sexual abuse of her.

She was living in India when she was pregnant with her son. She was infected by a parasite that had seriously weakened her. The delivery did not go well. She lost consciousness, and it became dark. Then her NDE started in the usual way.

She floated outside her body up to the ceiling from where she could see a great consternation unfolding around her body. She continued floating. She floated out the hospital and came to rest in a "dense, velvet-black space" in which she felt at ease. There was nothing there, but she felt free from all pain and fear, enveloped in a profound sense of peace and tranquility.

She had no body, but no pain, either. Time did not exist. Moreover, she realized that she was thinking and, therefore, that she must still exist. She knew it was real. She wrote that it was as true, as palpable, and as certain as had been my life on Earth . . . I was remembering something I had forgotten, something that had been erased from memory when I was born. (Thornton, 2014, pp. 94–95)

What she had forgotten was that she already existed before her life on Earth began, that is, before her birth into her current lifetime. She had returned to her source, which she recognized as her real home (Anonymous., 2013, June 17).

Swallowed Effortlessly Into the Light

Azmina Suleman was in the hospital due to what appeared to be an acute inflammation of the pancreas. In addition, her left lung had collapsed, her kidneys had failed, and she had gone into respiratory arrest. As the medics were trying to save her, she left her body.

In her wonderful book, *A Passage to Eternity*, she wrote compellingly about the multi-dimensional plane on the other side of life. But the first step was leaving her body:

It felt decidedly odd to be looking down upon myself in this dreamy and befuddled sort of way. It was like watching a three-dimensional movie of myself in which I could see myself lying on the bed, limp and lifeless like a piece of meat. I could also see the doctors and nurses fervently trying to resuscitate me back to life. But for some reason I felt a strange sense of detachment from the scene below. I just could not seem to identify with the seriousness of the situation, not get emotionally drawn into the drama of it all. After all, the "real" or essential me floated near the ceiling . . . I felt perfectly fine—even if a little wobbly.

As I hung around near the doorframe, I noticed that this lighter, gravity-defying version of myself even wore the same blue hospital gown with its grossly inadequate coverage that left a lot to be desired! However, I soon got bored of my surroundings and lost interest in the scene below. Like a bird that had suddenly been released from captivity, I suddenly yearned to roam the wide blue skies and explore my horizons . . . I found myself going through the hospital roof like a knife through butter. . . .

It was dark and hazy outside. I could just vaguely make out the dark silhouettes of some trees in the distance against what appeared to be a moonless sky. As I stood there in my bare feet wondering what to do next, I suddenly became aware of an intensely bright light in the sky directly ahead of me . . . The light shone out like a beacon. I felt like a winged moth relentlessly drawn towards the bright glow of a solitary lamp. And just for that split-second of a moment, it was as though time stood still. I could almost taste eternity . . . And before I knew it, I found myself being swallowed effortlessly into the light that easily outshone a thousand noonday suns . . . Once inside what was actually a narrow tunnel of light, I was immediately enveloped in a soothing cocoon of warmth . . . I was traveling what appeared to be the speed of light itself. It was like riding into eternity on the gossamer wings of light. (Suleman, 2004, pp. 12–14)

Mother of Pearl

At 13 years of age, this young experiencer went for a swim with friends. They didn't know the water was ice cold. The experiencer was the first to dive in and recounted a typical start of the NDE:

I was off to the other end, swimming like hell as I realized how freaking cold it was. All of a sudden, after a few numbing strokes, something happened. The cold was gone, and I was swimming in a cloud, and it was easy, as easy as I have ever known anything in my life, but a lot easier than that. I mean it was like my body was perfect, and I was flying, and it was unbelievably easy and very, very comfortable. The cloud was iridescent white, like mother of pearl, and as I moved forward it got brighter and brighter. It was so bright and so white, yet my eyes were not bothered by it in the least, it was perfect. I kept moving forward as I felt I was being drawn to something, and all I knew is that I wanted to go there. (Anonymous, 2004, March 4, 9:06 PM)

NO PAIN, BUT TOTAL PEACE AND SERENITY

Hands Around My Neck

Inevitably, some NDEs are associated with serious violence. As a young girl of eight, Christina was abducted by two men. One of them took her to a river's edge to drown her. She said that she gave up fighting and surrendered, causing her body to go into "freeze" mode.

He put his hands around my neck and held me under the water facing up. I remember seeing the sun from under the water and feeling an incredible sense of panic, which, within seconds, was replaced with an unlimited amount of peace and serenity. I then found myself in a very narrow tunnel of an incredibly bright white light. I was on my back floating and moving forward, feet first. I recall feelings of absolute bliss, and trying to describe this blissfulness with words would fail to measure up to this experience. . . . (Anonymous, 2012, November 18)

Christina told me that as she was drowning, she saw her parents far away working on the sailboat as if she was looking down on them from the sky above her body. She even saw her dad running in her direction because he heard her screams. After he resuscitated her and she had come to—she doesn't recall what had happened to the men—she immediately became very depressed, even suicidal—because she came back to this earthly environment after having been in a place she called "home."

Perfectly Fabulous

Yazmine Star was in the hospital for treatment related to a miscarriage. When two nurses took her to another floor for further internal examinations, her NDE began.

> Then suddenly I was above my body, which lay on a stretcher, wearing a white hospital gown. I looked at my body and knew it wasn't the real me: It was the thing I had been caught inside, and now I was free! Oh, and how I felt such happiness! . . . and the nurses were calling my name, one was crying tears, another was saying "Oh, my God, we've lost her!" Meanwhile I was above them thinking, "what silly Billy's, making all that fuss," wondering why they couldn't see me, and then to know that all was perfectly fabulous! (*Yazmine S NDE*, n.d.)

TUNNEL OR CAVE OR . . .

Stopped Worrying

Samieh was nine years old, on a trip with her parents. In the middle of the summer in a hot car without air conditioning, she had an absence seizure and stopped breathing.

> [I was] in a cave-like place. It was so dark. I thought it was odd that I was standing on nothing. I asked so many questions, but no one answered. I remember wondering if it was a prison or something. I was so confused. Then, I saw

a bright light at the end of this place. The light was very pleasant, and I stopped worrying about where I was or what was going to happen. (*Samieh NDE*, n.d.)

I Watched Myself Tumble

Rachel Finch was in the hospital, having lost a huge amount of blood during the delivery of her baby. Days later, she received a blood transfusion that did not seem to go well, and she passed out.

My eyes were so heavy, so I let them rest, and then I was up. I briefly hovered over my newborn baby, hoped she'd remember me, then I was travelling.

It felt like I was shooting through a tunnel, but I couldn't see any sides to it. It was dark, but illuminated. I was not alone. I could sense a presence with me. I was tumbling, forward/upward at an unfathomable speed. It felt like wind. All throughout me. Inside of me. I likened it at that age to being on a roller-coaster, that rushing feeling. It was wonderful. I felt so light, so free. Simultaneously, I experienced this fully and watched myself experience this with clear vision from a little distance. I can still see myself tumbling, if I concentrate on the memory. . . .

We traveled through the illuminated darkness until I saw a pinpoint of light in the distance.

When I saw it, it was like a "remembering." I knew where I was headed and I wanted to get there, fast. I can't recall if I was moving myself towards it or if I was being "drawn" to it somehow, but it was a "need/desire" within me. (Anonymous, 2019, June 10)

Tunnel Traveled With Him

Working on a ladder, Caan lost his balance. He fell backwards, headfirst, landing on concrete. He said that he heard the bones in my neck popping upon impact. At almost the same time my mind and body seemed to separate momentarily. (*Caan S NDE*, n.d.)

Then, as many other NDErs have done, he traveled at a high speed through a tunnel. However, unlike other NDErs have described, the tunnel traveled with him at the same high speed.

Eye of a Hurricane

During a thunderstorm, Dannion Brinkley (2008) was on a landline telephone when, through it, he was struck by lightning. Although it is amazing what he experienced when all that high voltage electricity went rushing through his body into the ground, at this point it is important to note *how* he arrived in that other world. Sometimes people report moving through a tunnel. In Dannion's case there was also a tunnel, but it is fascinating how he discovered it.

Dannion was outside his body, looking at it, and he knew he was dead. That was strange enough, but he also discovered that he could feel the sense of failure of the paramedic from the ambulance at not having been able to resuscitate his patient. Then just above his own body, Dannion saw that

a tunnel was forming, opening like the eye of a hurricane and coming towards me. (p. 6)

He said that *he* didn't move, rather the tunnel moved. It approached him with the sound of chimes and then swirled around him. Then, as has been the case with so many other NDErs, he moved forward through the tunnel and saw a light that became bigger as he approached it (pp. 5–7).

The Air Was Disrupted

Ellen Dye (2023) described how, during her NDE,

It suddenly occurred to me that most of the people I'd read about who had had near-death experiences reported seeing a great Light, often in the form of a wormhole or tunnel, and I wondered where the Light was. As the thought entered my mind, I felt rather than saw the Tunnel of Light. It was as if the air itself was suddenly disrupted by an amazingly wonderful energy, a feeling of amazing love and joy. The Light itself was bright and inviting and I effortlessly moved toward it . . . I felt it pulsing with love, and it called me, drew me, pulled me, and beckoned me . . . Home.

They Are You

Rachel Finch had a very deep NDE, which, like so many NDErs, she found very difficult to put into words, as the experience is ineffable. For that reason, she chose to write down her whole experience in *verse* in her book *Conversations With My Higher Self* (Finch, 2019). This is the first time I have seen an experience expressed this way, and I find the result astonishingly beautiful and very impressive. Another beautiful example of an NDE expressed in poetry is from Andrew Petro (2011). Rachel also submitted her NDE to the International Association for Near-Death Studies (IANDS) archives (Anonymous, 2019, June 10).

In the tunnel she had the feeling she wasn't alone; others were present.

I am in a dark, translucent tunnel, a thin veil of film
separating me from the vastness and I am aware of
other beings.
I think to myself, who are they and a quiet voice
within me murmurs,
they are you. (Finch, 2019, p. 33)

19

Been Here Hundreds of Times

While giving birth to her daughter, Brigitte Buyle (n.d.) had a hemorrhage and died. In a fantastic interview for Ponto3.org, she told her story. She came out of her body and suddenly sat against the wall looking at her body in the bed. At the same time, she was elsewhere:

> I found myself near a very old staircase somewhere, and I thought, "Oh, no." I knew right away, I'm dying, because that staircase, or that road, let's say it was a staircase, I don't know, well, yes, a staircase. I thought, I've been here already hundreds of times, have seen it hundreds of times. I just knew, "Ah yes, it's the way back again" . . . it was so familiar, so familiar, so familiar, like I've walked past it every day for years, so you really know all the details.

—— HAVING A NON-PHYSICAL FORM ——

I don't know how long I had been unconscious before I realized that I had left my body on the couch and was looking down at it through the ceiling. It meant no more to me than an old coat that I had discarded. There was no fear or confusion, just a wonderful weightlessness and freedom.

I was aware of having a form of some kind that was not physical but felt perfectly natural. I turned my attention away from the scene below, which seemed to be receding and getting smaller, and found myself in a velvety, dark stillness. I wanted to move through it but couldn't. I was blocked. Then I felt a protective, yet powerful presence, and words came to me in a voice that was not a voice. I have no way to describe it; telepathy is as close as I can get. It said, "It's not your time. You must go back." I didn't want to, even though at that time I had everything to live for. I was newly engaged, buying a house, and my career was taking off. (Anonymous, 2010, December 20, 17:04)

TWO POINTS OF VIEW

In a fantastic book, *Awakenings From the Light*, Nancy Rynes (2015) wrote about her two impressive NDEs. She had her first NDE while she was cycling in her town and was run over by an SUV. Her second, very deep NDE happened three days later, during the operation required to reconstruct her spine. About her first NDE, she wrote:

> In human time, this NDE lasted just a few minutes. As I was struck, I realized that my consciousness was in two places simultaneously. One part, very scared and animal-like, was firmly inside of my broken body that was stuck on the vehicle's axle and being dragged under the truck. The other part, a very calm, dispassionate observer, hovered out in front of the truck and off to the south, watching the whole scene unfold from a distance. This dual consciousness seemed quite normal to the observer part of me. The observer was calm about the whole thing, and I remember the feeling that this was all happening for a reason, that there was nothing to fear. The observer—me—watched as witnesses stopped . . . and called for help . . . When the paramedics started working on [my body], my two selves came back together. (*Nancy R NDE*, n.d.; Rynes, 2015, pp. 3–11)

BEAUTIFUL COLORS

In her marvelous book *While I Was Out . . . God Came In*, Deirdre DeWitt Maltby (2012) described how she felt the right tire of her car go off the pavement onto the shoulder of the road. There was a loud thud and a bang, after which her car started to spin and was hit by a semi-truck. Her car rolled several times before slamming into a hill. She was taken to the hospital ICU where her NDE began.

She started to see a beautiful essence of yellow that comforted her. At first, she thought it was a new way of comforting patients, but then she noticed that she could see 360 degrees in all directions. Because of this ability, she realized that she was no longer attached to her body.

> This is hard to explain because I have been attached to my physical body my whole life. Feeling the ability to exist without a body is quite difficult to describe in full. It was not like being awake within a dream; it was being conscious in another type of reality . . . This experience seemed outside of time . . . I was then gently pulled or guided through what I perceived to be many thousands of colors. This new adventure all started slowly, one beautiful color at a time. Each color got more vivid or intense than the last, and the colors then magically changed shades from within . . . The alluring colors were not flat, but three-dimensional; the sounds seemed three-dimensional as well. The experience was close to indescribable, at least in Earthly terms . . . colors, music, and thoughts mystically all became *one*. . . .'

Then there was this feeling of "all-encompassing" whiteness:

> This white was totally pure, blindly brilliant, yet it felt very welcoming. It was pureness itself, in a raw and ultimate form. MY soul immediately knew it *was* the center of the Universe. (pp. 42–47)

Another NDEr, Catja de Rijk (2021), described similarly:

22

The tunnel . . . had such beautiful soft colors that flowed into each other . . . What I felt there, I have never, never experienced here on Earth! (p. 31)

I COULD SEE EVERYBODY

In her wonderful book, *Crossing Over & Coming Home*, containing 21 insightful cases of gay NDErs, Liz Dale (2008) wrote about a man who had a cycling accident. He suddenly saw his body lying on the pavement. He was totally amazed by this sight because it was the first time that he saw himself three-dimensionally.

It was such a shock, because we usually never see ourselves except in a one-dimensional mirror reflection, or a photograph. But I felt no pain at all. I felt completely whole and free, and I thought, "This is who I really am." (p. 90)

Then, after a little bit of time, he took off. He felt himself being pulled away from the Earth, at the speed of light.

I saw all of the people on the planet simultaneously in that one moment. I saw people in China and Sweden and Uruguay. I saw people sleeping and dreaming. I saw people preparing food in their homes and restaurants . . . I saw mothers giving birth to children, which was especially beautiful and moving to me. (p. 90)

LOSING ATTACHMENT

Anita Moorjani (2012) has written a fantastic book, *Dying to Be Me*, about her NDE, which she had when she was dying of cancer. She described the extraordinary moment when she slipped out of her body. She felt the deep grief of her husband and mother, both of whom were by her bed. At the same time, she felt herself being pulled out of that situation. She felt her attachment to her family and everything else fade. She wrote:

> As my emotions were being drawn away from my surroundings, I started to notice how I was continuing to expand to fill every space, until there was no separation between me and everything else. I encompassed—no, *became*—everything and everyone. (p. 64)

She said that it was a kind of "awakening." She expanded far beyond her own body and physical world.

> My soul was finally realizing its true magnificence! (p. 65)

CHAPTER 2

Veridical Observations

To prove scientifically that NDEs are a first real step into an afterlife is extremely difficult. The reason is that we need tests that can be repeated independently by others and yield the same or a similar outcome. The problem with NDEs is that they occur unexpectedly and cannot be repeated in a controlled test environment.

However, there might be another way to come close to proving that NDEs provide a true glimpse of what awaits us humans after death. One category of such evidence involves the very first moments of an NDE in which the experiencer finds oneself at a location outside the physical body, perceiving the material world. In some cases, NDErs have made observations that could be verified and corroborated later. The observations were *veridical*. Many such cases have been published, and their number is growing. A great book has been published in its second edition, now with over 125 of these verified cases: *The Self Does Not Die* (Rivas et al., 2023).

When contemplating the relationship of mind and brain, veridical cases should be considered seriously. In my opinion, these cases, taken together, provide strong evidence that consciousness can exist independent of the brain. And as such, these cases point to some certainty about a life after death.

——— THE MAN WITH THE DENTURES ———

The case of "the man with the dentures" is mentioned in the research of cardiologist Pim van Lommel which was published in the highly rated medical journal *Lancet* (van Lommel et al., 2001). A man was found in a Dutch meadow suffering a massive heart attack. During the ambulance ride, several resuscitation attempts were made. In the hospital, the three nurses who took over the resuscitation noticed that in addition to no heart rate or blood circulation, the patient was not breathing and had no noticeable consciousness. His features were gray, and he seemed already to have postmortem lividity.

In the process of trying to intubate the patient with an artificial respirator, one of the nurses, a man, found that the patient was wearing a set of false teeth. He removed the dentures and put them on a wooden shelf of the crash cart. At that time in 1979, crash carts were not as common as they are now. This particular cart was modified from an ordinary kitchen cart. Therefore, it was both primitive and unique. The resuscitation took about an hour, which is quite long for this procedure, but eventually was successful. The nurse went home and had a weeklong vacation.

When the nurse returned from vacation, his schedule was to attend to patients, amongst whom was the patient he had helped resuscitate. Even though the patient had been unconscious upon entering the hospital, during the entire resuscitation, and even for some time after his heartbeat had been restored, he immediately recognized the nurse. To the amazement of the nurse, the patient was able to tell him where he had put the patient's dentures. The patient said he had been hovering close to the ceiling and had seen everything that happened— the entire procedure. He could describe the room, even the recessed sink, which he could not have seen from where he was lying while in that room. He also described the crash cart, where the medical team, in fact, actually found his dentures (Coppes, 2011, pp. 46–47).

OPERATION STANDSTILL

This is the well-known case of a young woman with swelling in one of the main blood vessels in her brain. It was featured in a BBC documentary, *The Day I Died*, which is available for viewing online (Broome, 2002). This particular swelling can be pictured like a bubble on the side of a defective bicycle tire. Because of its location deep in the brain and the risk that, during the typical brain surgery used at that time, the swelling would burst and the patient would die, the condition was considered inoperable. Fortunately for this woman, just at that time, a radical new surgical procedure, known as hypothermic cardiac arrest, was being developed. The nickname of this operation, "standstill," is clearer than the medical term and illustrates exactly what the procedure involves.

The patient's body was cooled to a temperature of 60 degrees Fahrenheit (about 15 degrees Celsius), her breathing and heartbeat were stopped, her brain waves flattened to zero, and all blood was drained from her head. All of this was done to reduce the size of the swelling, as if the air was being taken out of a defective tire. In this manner, the deflated bubble could much more easily be excised and removed. Then everything was reversed: blood returned to the head, the body returned to normal temperature, and heart restarted.

During the entire surgery, which lasted about an hour and 25 minutes, the patient was very carefully monitored. While she was fully anesthetized, her eyes were closed and taped, and her ears were plugged, she experienced that she was pulled out of the top of her head. She later told that a particular sound pulled her out. It was "a frequency that you go on," as if it was a road. That was the start of a very deep NDE. In the first portion of it, she experienced her consciousness functioning clearly outside her body, and she accurately saw details of the surgical procedures and instruments. As if she was sitting on the surgeon's shoulder, she said, she had a brighter, more focused and clearer vision of everything that was happening than she would have had if she were seeing with her physical eyes. She had expected that the nurses would have shaved all her hair off for the operation, but they had not done so.

Before entering the operating room, she could not have seen the instruments that were going to be used, because they were kept in their packaging and covered for hygienic reasons—opened only at the point during surgery that they would be used. Nevertheless, she would later give a good description of the bone saw—used to drill into her skull. She said that it looked like an electric toothbrush and that it had interchangeable blades.

Her ears had been plugged with speakers that emitted 100-decibel clicks in one ear and white noise in the other, with the team switching the two sounds periodically to prevent deafness. By continuously plying the patient with this loud noise, they could detect when the brain was not responding even to this intrusive stimulation, showing that the patient was completely flatlined. Despite being fully anesthetized along with the complete plugging of her ears and the loud noise from the speakers in them, she later reported that she overheard the conversation between her brain surgeon and the cardiac surgeon about how the veins on one side of her groin were too small to be connected to the heart-lung machine that would store her drained blood and keep it viable during the surgery. She also described the bone saw's sound as being high-pitched and how suddenly "it went brrrrrrrr."

All of this happened while the team was cooling her body and before blood had been drained from it. The cardiac surgeon found a usable vein, and the standstill procedure progressed. Eventually, while monitored closely by the medical team, she had no heartbeat, blood pressure, or respiration, and her brain waves flattened, indicating that the brain had totally shut down. She remained in this clinically dead condition for over an hour while her surgeon excised the aneurysm. At the point when her blood was drained from her body, "like oil from a car," she said, she was pulled away from the operating room scene. It was not against her will, she said later; it was of her own accord. She went through a tunnel where she heard her grandmother calling her. Subsequently, she saw the Light, and finally she saw many other deceased people in this Light, amongst them, her grandmother. Even though all the spirits were friendly, they would not permit her to go any further. She had to go back and, fortunately, that was also what she desired for herself, because she wanted to look after her children. She was told that if she would go any further into the Light, returning would no longer be possible.

> Something would happen to me physically. They would be unable to put this ME back into the body ME, like I had gone too far, and they couldn't reconnect. So they wouldn't let me go anywhere or do anything.

Her reentry into her body also was interesting. Her uncle—who was physically deceased but, in this domain, very much alive—guided her back through the tunnel. At the end, she saw "the thing, my body." She didn't want to get back into it. Her uncle gently pushed her into that thing, and it felt "like diving into a pool of ice water" (Coppes, 2011, pp. 47–50; Rivas et al., 2023, pp. 114–123; Sabom, 1998, pp. 37–52).

THE FLAPPING SURGEON

Al Sullivan's first-person NDE account is available online (Javier, n.d.). Al was totally convinced that he was not out of his mind, but only out of his body. During an examination at the hospital, one of his coronary arteries became blocked. He had to undergo immediate surgery.

In the operating room, Dr. Takata introduced himself as the cardiovascular surgeon. He said that they would take veins from his legs and elsewhere and create four or five bypasses. Meanwhile, Al was given anesthesia.

> I am listening and listening. And all of a sudden, I don't have to listen to him telling me. I can *see* what he is doing because I found out that I wasn't there to listen anymore. I just left my body and watched. I can see, but I am up, looking down at what used to be me. It wasn't me, because the real me is up here, watching. That is when they started putting stuff over my eyes and all kinds of drapes and blankets all around me. And, still, I can see Dr. Takata and his people. And this is another thing, I could see through the operating table and me, and I could see what kind of boots he had on. At one point he stepped back. The surgeon stepped back. And it looked like he was flapping his arms. And I—what in the world is he doing that for? He was orchestrating, do this, do that, and it did seem very foreign to me what he was doing.

From a physical perspective, Al Sullivan could not possibly have seen the doctor perform the operation, his arms flapping about. During the operation Al's eyes were taped, and a sterile drape would make it impossible for him to use his physical eyes to see anything the doctor did. However, this part of the operation was not the only part that Al Sullivan could describe; there were more parts that he could relate in detail.

This case is special because the medical staff contacted NDE researcher and psychiatrist Bruce Greyson soon after the surgery ended. They did this after the patient was taken to post-op where he had regained consciousness and immediately told the staff what he had experienced. Greyson promptly investigated the case. In that investigation, he learned the explanation of the "flapping" elbows. When Dr. Takata was not actually operating, he did not want to contaminate his hands, so he would rest them on the sterile gown covering his chest, and he would use his elbows to point and instruct his assistants what to do.

Dr. Takata later acknowledged, "I cannot explain how he saw these things under the complete sleep of anesthesia." In the account of this case in the book *The Self Does Not Die* (Rivas et al., 2023, pp. 9–11), Dr. Takata stated that he was aware of cases in which the anesthetic wears off during the operation and the patient hears the doctor's conversation. He also wrote that he has had such patients. He then went on:

> But I have never encountered one in which the patient describes such details of the operation as if he/she saw the process. Frankly, I don't know how this case can be accounted for. But since this really happened, I have to accept it as a fact. I think we should always be humble to accept the fact. In sum, I think science has not yet sufficiently revealed the ability of human beings. There exists in this world something that cannot be captured by science or mathematics. (Javier, n.d.)

SMOKING GRANNIES

Michaela can be seen online telling her story (Garrett, B., n.d.). In 1994, at age 17, she was the victim of a serious car collision with a heavy truck. Her injuries were so serious that she was taken by helicopter to the nearest hospital. She had suffered severe brain injury. During the flight she slipped into a coma, and she had her NDE, including a very detailed life review. She also had a preview of her future life in which she saw she would have grandchildren of her own.

In her NDE she was loved and hugged by "God or her higher self," and the feeling was great. She could die if she wanted, but then she couldn't lead the happy life that she had seen with her grandchildren. Then she pleaded with God not to let her die. She cried, prayed, and fought, and then:

> All of a sudden, it felt like being sucked out of space in this tube or something, it was just like a vacuum . . . Next thing that I know, I was up in the corner of the hospital room looking at my body that lay there. (Garrett, B., n.d.)

Her family had gathered around her, and they were sad. She tried to comfort them, but, of course, they didn't hear her. She says that she could move freely around the hospital and that she was in and out of her body for about a week and a half. That ability in itself is quite remarkable, but the most interesting part of her story is when, during her NDE, she saw her mom and dad in a cafeteria in the hospital.

> It was like a bench style seating. And my grandma and gran were sitting across from my parents. And my dad is a smoker, and he said he was gonna go have a cigarette because he just wanted to give them some breathing room and get out of there. And it is funny, because my grandmother there, my mom's mom, who had never or would never have a cigarette in her life, was like: "Oh, I want one, too. I'm gonna have one, too." Then my other

grandma said, "me too." And neither of my grandmas
would ever smoke a cigarette.' (Rivas et al. 2023, p. 53;
Garrett, B., n.d.)

Later her parents didn't believe any of the things she told them
about this episode of wandering about in the hospital—until
she told the story of the smoking grannies.

THE BLUE TENNIS SHOE

During a resuscitation, a patient floated out of her body
towards a ledge outside the hospital. There she saw a tennis
shoe, which had some detailed characteristics like the color
(dark blue), a wear spot over the little toe, and the Nike logo.
Later the patient asked a social worker to see if there actually
was such a shoe in the ledge. The social worker, Kimberly Clark
Sharp, did indeed find the shoe. Since the publication of this
story, skeptics have tried to downplay it, but Kimberly has
addressed the criticism point by point. I know Kimberly personally, and, in my opinion, she is not only very warmhearted
but also very trustworthy. Read her own side of the story in
her book *After the Light*. There you will also read about her
own NDE she had years before she found the tennis shoe—and
about what she discovered on the other side that may change
your life (Rivas et al., 2023, pp. 40–43; Sharp, 2003, pp. 7–14;
Sharp, 2007).

THE GREAT RECESSION

This is a story from my own research, and even though it
might not qualify as a pure veridical observation, it still indicates that some truth lies in NDEs.

When the Great Recession (2007–2009) was only in its
first phase, I had one of my interviews with an NDEr. The

crisis had started in August 2007 and lingered on until Bear Stearns, one of the major investment banks, was running into serious problems. I spoke with the NDEr in March 2008, right after Bear Stearns had been saved by JP Morgan/Chase in a deal brokered by the Federal Reserve. Everyone was sighing with relief, and stock prices quickly recovered from their previous losses.

While people were scrambling to buy stocks again, the NDEr told me that this episode with Bear Stearns was just the beginning. She said:

> **What is happening in America is just the forerunner of the real crisis. The real crisis is still to come, and it will really be severe.**

She had been given this information in 1986 during her NDE, but she didn't understand it because it came in an elevated form of communication. The knowledge became intangible after her experience. In addition, she is not knowledgeable about finance, and for that reason alone she was not able to explain what she had seen. However, the turmoil that started in 2007, which led to the fearful tension preceding the Bear Sterns rescue, made her understand that this was the time frame that she had seen in 1986. Her feelings during the NDE matched the fearful tension she sensed in the world of March 2008.

At the time of the interview, I didn't really give much thought to what she was saying. I made my notes and went on with my life—until September of that year. The two gigantic mortgage enterprises, Fannie Mae and Freddie Mac, and the biggest insurance company in the world, AIG, ran into mounting problems. Until that moment, the failure of these three mammoth financial firms had not been thought possible. Finally, they had to be saved by the U.S. Treasury by being wholly or partly nationalized. Then in mid-September 2008, Lehman Brothers, another investment bank, went bankrupt, which triggered the gradual breakdown of the financial system as we had known it since World War II. It led to the full or partial nationalization of many more banks and insurance companies in Europe and the US. The breakdown of the financial system caused the most severe economic crisis the world had experienced since the Great Depression of the 1930s.

So, as it turned out, she had been right (Coppes, 2011, pp. 144–145).

NEUROSCIENTIST

This story is not strictly an example of a veridical observation, but it is so special that I want to include it in this chapter, nonetheless. Like the preceding and following stories, it does have aspects that were verified after the experience.

During the 2011 IANDS conference in Durham, North Carolina, neuroscientist Eben Alexander III first spoke about his own NDE, which was later published in his brilliant bestseller *Proof of Heaven* (Alexander, 2012) and summarized on his website (Alexander, n.d.). He had been a member of the Harvard University medical school faculty, and as an academic neurosurgeon over the previous 25 years, he had treated many comatose patients. He said he thought he knew pretty much everything there was to know about the brain and consciousness. He saw himself as a "materialist": someone who thinks the brain determines consciousness.

In November 2008, he himself fell into a coma due to an extremely rare case of spontaneous *E. coli* meningitis. What then happened to him changed his materialist view of the world.

Before I tell you his story, you need to know that Alexander was adopted as a baby in 1954. Because his son, Eben

IV, wanted to compile his family tree for a project at school in 1999, the senior Alexander wrote to the children's home, from which he had been adopted, to ask if there was any information about his biological family. At first, he was told that his parents had been very much in love with each other but that they had each gone their own way. His mother could not take care of him, and so he ended up in the orphanage.

In a second communication, in February 2000, he was told that his biological parents had eventually married and that they had three more children. Unfortunately, the youngest daughter had just passed away. He was also told that it was not a good time to come back into their lives, because they were still grieving the loss of their youngest daughter—which shocked him. Over the next few years, however, he *did* manage to make contact with them.

Eight years later, during his meningitis-related coma, he had an NDE in which he experienced a reality that was more real than the earthly reality he had known up to that time. It was very vibrant. He said that his consciousness was at a fundamental level. He was in an exceptionally beautiful landscape in absolute harmony. There were splashing waterfalls, barking dogs, beautiful music, and a lovely warm summer breeze.

As he was flying through that wonderful landscape on a butterfly wing, he noticed a stunningly beautiful and remarkable woman seated next to him. The communication with her was not in words, yet it was very direct. She radiated unconditional love.

In the final stages of his journey, he witnessed six faces that served as veridical time anchors, linking the earthly presence of family and loved ones in the ICU with events in his NDE. The final face, that of a ten-year-old boy, was what finally drew him back to this world. It was the face of his son, Bond, pleading with him to be present. Even though he did not recognize Bond in that moment, their strong loving connection and the sense Eben had of his responsibility to be there for Bond ultimately brought him back to this world.

And he did go back. In the months following his miraculous recovery, he continued to wonder who the stunningly beautiful and lovely young woman in his NDE was. After four months of recovery, his biological family had decided to send him a photo of the youngest daughter who had died as an adult—his sister. When he saw the photo, he said it was as if he'd been punched in the gut, collapsing to the floor and unable to stand for many minutes. The woman in the photo turned out to be that gorgeously beautiful and loving woman in his NDE. It could only mean that he had met his deceased sister—without ever having known in physical life who she was or that she had died!

It therefore became clear to him that NDEs are real experiences, and they also present an awkward problem for neuroscience. He told me that many of his fellow neurosurgeons are slowly but surely beginning to admit that, like most people who have studied NDEs, they don't really know how to explain this phenomenon and are less sure of their materialist worldview than before.

———— SHARED DEATH EXPERIENCE ————

Mother and Child Reunion

Scott Taylor's (n.d.) girlfriend and her 7-year-old son were in a serious car accident. She died, and her son had received a severe head injury and was also expected to die soon. The family and Scott were together in the hospital room when the boy transitioned. Scott said that he saw his girlfriend come down

> and [she] scooped [her son] out of his body, and it was an exquisite reunion. That reunion was filled with joy—you can only imagine a mother receiving her son back again.

But then a really, quite extraordinary thing happened. They turned to me and included me in their embrace, and then the three of us went to The Light together. This was something I could never have possibly imagined because when we hit The Light, when we entered this Light, it was joy, this amazing love, it was this bursting of reunion with the most loving entities and with [the mother] and [her son].

Slowly he returned to the hospital room. He thought it inappropriate to talk to the others about his experience of this bilocation. However, 15 years later, Scott interviewed a woman who had had an NDE and who also had been present in that hospital room. During the interview, he discovered that when the boy passed, she had had nearly the identical experience as Scott:

That she had witnessed [the mother] come and pick [her son] out of his body. That she had witnessed the same exquisite reunion between [the mother] and [her son]. And that [the mother] and [her son] had turned to her and taken her to The Light.

Fiancée

The story below is not an example of a veridical observation, but it shows that shared death experiences like Scott's have occurred to other people. This is a story of a Vietnamese boy, Vu Tran. At the age of 15 in 1975, just before the establishment of communism in South Vietnam, he emigrated to the US with his parents and siblings. He became socially successful and believed that he was the master of his destiny—that nobody and nothing could change it.

One night, returning from a short vacation, he was in the car with his fiancée—neither of them wearing seatbelts.

I remember turning over to look at my fiancée and catching her smile. I turned back and suddenly saw the headlights. It was a horrific head-on collision, and miraculously I was the sole survivor. I had a near-death experience because I saw my fiancée going toward a bright light, and I just followed her. But as she entered this bright light, she turned around and told me, "You cannot come because you still have something to do!" After she said it, I immediately felt the heaviness and found myself in pain with blood on my body. I saw her resting on the passenger-side dashboard. I reached over and brought her back on the chair. . . . Later . . . the ER doctor came to tell me that there was nothing they could do to save my fiancée because she suffered a massive brain injury. (Anonymous, 2021, July 8)

CHAPTER 3

Out of This World

NDEs are extraordinary experiences. People who have had an NDE speak of a world that is completely different from the world we know. It seems to be a non-material world with unearthly landscapes, colors, sounds, look, and feel. It is more beautiful than our world. It is more dimensional. It is a world in which space and time are completely different. Space and time even seem non-existent, nor do they form obstacles as they do in our world: It seems that in the transmaterial dimension, we can be wherever we want to be and in whatever time we choose. Our deceased friends and relatives are there, and even our deceased pets. Communication with them, with other beings of light, or with the Light itself is effortless. And we know whatever there is to know because all knowledge is freely available.

This is something that baffles NDErs' minds. Nevertheless, according to NDErs it is a world that truly exists. Many of them even say that that world is more real than our world.

In most NDEs, love plays an important role. It is not just love, but it is LOVE—with capital letters. It is love of the unconditional kind; there are simply no conditions to receiving this love. Most NDErs say that this love is the most important thing they feel on the other side of earthly life. It is there for all of us, for each one of us individually, and there are no exceptions.

Love also seems to be the most important thing in our earthly world, because our world is somehow a part of that other world. The other world is very close. We can perhaps compare it to the situation where we are locked up in the bathroom of the palace, but we are in the palace, nonetheless. It is all around us, but we can't see it. We will be released from the bathroom (so to speak), and be able to see the wonders of the rest of the palace. . . .

Some NDErs say that this other world is not only around us, but that it is superimposed on our world. However, for one or another reason, we fail to see it.

That we can't see it doesn't mean it does not exist. NDErs are convinced it is there—and that they will return to that other world after their physical death. This is the reason why so many NDErs aren't afraid of dying.

In this chapter you will find many quotes of NDErs to show how different this other world is. Don't read the quotes hastily as if you need to catch a train. Do it slowly. Do it one by one, so you can savor how extraordinary and out-of-our-world this other world is.

And don't think that these quotes are nonsensical or impossible, and that they are too extreme to give us a good impression of that other reality. Just set aside what you have learned during your life in our four-dimensional, space-time world, because it could well be that this other world has more dimensions than ours.

Our earthly world has four space-time dimensions, and it is difficult to imagine a world with more than these four dimensions. Even if it is only one extra dimension, it would be something we would never be able to understand or describe with our current concepts.

Let's do an experiment—based on 19th century author Edwin Abbott's book, *Flatland*. Just imagine a world with one dimension less than our own world: rather than four—length, width, height, and time—only three—no height.

A three-dimensional world would be a world where flat (two-dimensional) people live who have knowledge of time (the third dimension). If there were trees, they would be completely different from our trees because they would be flat as well.

Flat people can walk around a flat tree but, by definition, can never climb it. They wouldn't even know the concept of climbing because height does not exist in their flat world.

Should we step onto this flat world and walk over it, flat people would see only where we put our feet. For them, something would suddenly appear, then disappear again, and then suddenly emerge once more a little further on. They would have no idea what it is and would never be able to describe exactly what it is. They would perhaps call it a ghost that would appear and disappear, or maybe a random moving apparition. In any case, they would have no idea whatsoever about the whole body, our body, that is attached to that moving apparition.

Now imagine that one of them was given a once-in-a-lifetime chance to glimpse our four-dimensional world. He would be completely bewildered, and upon returning to his flat world, would never be able to describe to his fellow flat people what he had seen. How could he ever express that these moving apparitions are just a minor part, or even just an imprint, of a whole body that is attached to it? He would say incomprehensible and cryptic things to his brothers and sisters, such as, "The other world is more real, you have more possibilities, you can move more freely, you can see in all directions at the same time, and even though we cannot see it, that world is all around us."

That is exactly what happens to NDErs. They struggle to find the right words to describe their experience. And they fail, because the right words aren't there. Language was developed to reflect our four-dimensional world, not that other, multi-dimensional world. In the language of this world, the experience of that other world is *ineffable.*

43

Before you read the quotes that show how extraordinary that other world is, remember that no two NDEs are the same. Each one is unique and different.

In addition, NDErs seem to have some control over their experience. It is not clear why this is, but it seems that we partly color our NDE ourselves. The images we get to see arise partly from our personal unconscious. They could also arise from our collective unconscious.

For example, people in Western cultures sometimes perceive Jesus or God in the Light, whereas people from other cultures see their God, or Gods, or important spiritual figures in the Light, from their own religious perspective. Some examples are Mohammad (*Halil T NDE*, n.d.), Kalika or Kali—the Hindu goddess who destroys evil (*Arvind B NDE*, n.d.), and Durga—the Hindu goddess of creation (*Neha S NDE*, n.d.).

All these differences need not alarm us, nor do they mean that NDEs are figments of the imagination. The fact that our consciousness can exist independently from our body is already apparent from veridical observations discussed in the previous chapter. What we need to do is to look at the central themes underlying all those differences: that there is an afterlife, that unconditional love is the building block of everything (Chapter 4), and that all of us are, at the minimum, closely connected to each other and to all that exists (Chapter 9).

⸺ IT IS GRAND AND SO VERY BEAUTIFUL ⸺

No Words in Our Language
When Carol Lynn Vengroff was 12 years old, she was in Paris. Her NDE occurred in one of the most severe winters, namely on the coldest night in France's recorded history in 1963. Heating and electricity were off, and she was in bed fully dressed including a coat and other outdoor clothing.

However, because of the terrible cold she drifted off into her NDE. She wrote a short book about her experience, *My Ever After Chronicles* (Vengroff, 2012) in which she wrote about all the wisdom she received and could take back to Earth. Even though it is a short book, it is filled with uplifting messages. She wrote about how different this environment was in which she suddenly found herself. She had a life review (see Chapter 6) and felt an overwhelming joy.

She wrote about this place that

> . . . there are no words in our human language that even came remotely close to being able to describe the dimension I had entered. . . . This was a place without time. Hours, minutes, seconds, night, day, months, years, centuries, eons did not exist. Yet, there was an order, a system to everything taking place. . . . All my senses were indescribably amplified and heightened in a way I had never experienced on earth. I felt real. I felt more alive, more than I could ever remember. (Vengroff, 2012, pp. 14–16)

Beethoven and Rembrandt

One of the best mediums I know is Anoeska Coopman in Amsterdam. Her mediumship gift has been further enhanced by her trip to 'headquarters,' as she calls the place where she was during her NDE. She is in the process of writing a book about her 'trip' and the spiritual path she is walking in her life. In an excerpt from her book, she talked about how difficult it is to put these overwhelming experiences into words, but also how important it is to look beyond the differences in NDEs and concentrate on the common messages:

> Hundreds of thousands of people have had a Near-Death Experience (or as I call it a Death Experience), a physically

and emotionally profound experience for all those people who have gone through it. These experiences often differ in detail, yet (with a few exceptions) they essentially talk about the same thing. Everyone experiences freedom, wisdom, love, and unity. My explanation for the differences in NDEs is the following: after coming back into the body, each brain tries to put flesh on the bones of the experience. To do this, the brain finds the best matching images from its memory that it can find. It tries to understand and translate something unearthly in an earthly way. Every person, so every memory, has a different "archive" of images in its fantasy. And every attempt to put that experience into words (involving everyone's individual vocabulary) leads to differences. Every unearthly experience is thus translated by an earthly body. That's impossible. Also, because there are no earthly words and comparable images, it's like playing Beethoven on a bucket, painting a Rembrandt on a paving stone with two colors of chalk . . . So, every translation will be different. If one foreign-language poem is translated by five interpreters, five different versions will appear. All five slightly different but all five with the same essentials. . . .

Center of All Places

After surviving a near-fatal assault, this person said it was nearly impossible to put the experience into words for the simple reason that there aren't enough suitable words and concepts in our human language to do so:

> I was in a place that is no place. It was the center of all places, outside the known universe (or our understanding of it) and encompassing the entire universe. (Anonymous, 2004, March 25, 9:14 PM)

Other NDErs have said something similar:

I had gotten only the slightest glimpse of the limitless realms beyond the finite boundaries of the world we inhabit. (Thornton, 2014, p. 98)

The experience was more real, more vivid, and more dimensional than living. (Anonymous, 2009, April 18)

Earth is an illusion created by the Light. Reality does not exist on Earth. Reality only exists within the Light. (Petro, 2014, locations 574, 610)

I felt freer and more alive than I ever had. (Moorjani, 2012, p. 66)

Heaven was so beautiful. It was as if all the colors on earth are in black and white, but in heaven they vibrate. (Dale, 2008, p. 33)

I Want to Have a CD of It

A man I interviewed, who wished to remain anonymous and used the pseudonym Noël de Waele, described his NDE this way:

I was in a large field of white light. It was inexpressible. I was there only with my consciousness because I had no body. Yet it was very real. The light that I saw there, that is my own divinity.

There was also wonderful music. The echo of the music resounded in my heart. It was a kind of harp music, very delicate and fragile. Immediately I thought: "I want to have it on CD." (Coppes, 2021/2022, p. 24)

SUPERIMPOSED

Sitting on Top of My Guardian

A small girl, only three years old, had a febrile seizure. The experience has always stayed with her because she seemed to be in two worlds at once.

> I was aware at all times of both the "real" world and the plane that the beings of light inhabited. In fact, the two worlds seemed to be super-imposed on one another. At times I could see my parents in the room with the priest, and he would sit on the chair right on top of one of my guardians. (Anonymous, 2013, July 19)

Floating Above the Real World

As a young woman, Jane Bannister left her body through the head and likened it to being born into another world.

> I became aware of another world, superimposed on the physical world. There was a boundary of parkland floating a few feet above the real grass.

She went on to explain:

> I floated out of my head of my dying anorexic body and could see the grass verge in front of the university halls of residence where my bed was. Floating a few feet above the grass was another patch of grass, on which stood several figures in grey cloaks and hoods. They were discussing me, and whether I should be allowed to live or not. It was as if both scenes [meaning the other patch of grass and the hooded figures] were slightly translucent, I could see them both at once almost solidly in color, and yet with just enough transparency to see the university

grounds through the patch of grass on which the figures stood. (Anonymous, 2010, December 20, 16:40)

TIME?

All time exists at once. (Taylor, 2001, p. 140)

It was not done in time; it was between time. (Taylor, 2001, pp. 73)

I was watching eternity unfold. (Sharp, 2003, p. 25)

I realized Time did no longer appear to me as it had in my body. It was as if I were projected into a moment, or dragged through time, backwards before forwards, to re-feel. (Anonymous [Rachel Finch], 2019, June 10)

From here on any concept of time just doesn't work anymore the way it does there. Time does not exist. (Anonymous, 2018, May 14)

Many Versions of the Earth

. . . there is no such thing as linear time on the Other Side. Everything is always experienced in the now, including past and future. . . . I was a part of the universe. I could see the earth towards my right but there were many versions of it. They were all following one after the other, forming a circle, and they were in various stages of evolution. There was no beginning or end to time and they (the earths) just seemed to be separate stages of one whole process. I was a part of the stars and although I did not have a physical body, I felt more real than ever before. (Anonymous [Juliet Nightingale], 2002, February 5, 1:18 PM)

All at Once

Something else that might be hard to comprehend is that there is no such thing as time! Your life is happening all at once, meaning your past/ present/ future are all one bubble. It's our brain (filter) that makes this so-called time linear. Huh? I know . . . strange! That might raise questions of "free will." Do we have it? Yes and no. Just because your life is predetermined, you don't know what the outcome will be. Things can change on a dime. Always remember that! I knew everything about the universe . . . why/ how/ what's the point of it all? I was there for so long it was hard not to know everything! When I returned, I couldn't remember a lot of information that I had received. I assumed it was intentional. (Anonymous, 2016, September 23)

Blocked From Me

There was no time in this place. Every moment of history and the present and the future were unfolded before me as one monumental event starting with the creation of the universe and ending, well that has since been blocked from me in such a way that it hurts to try to remember. (Anonymous, 2004, March 25, 9:14 PM)

View of Her Future Life

After a car accident, Geertrui Lagae had a very complete NDE. In an interview with Ponto3.org, she said she saw things that would happen in her future life and that did, indeed, happen:

It was more real than life itself. Yes, and also the realities that I saw there, which I could not see here. There I saw more realities that had happened here on Earth or were yet to happen. They did happen later in my life. So, it is more real, more factual. (Lagae, n.d.)

Car or Airplane

As a small child during World War II, Tienke Klein was imprisoned in a Japanese concentration camp in the then-colony of the Dutch East Indies. During the inhumanely harsh regimen in the concentration camp, she had her first NDE, and later in life she had a second one. She has written a moving book in Dutch about her experiences, *De Kiem*, which can be translated as *Essence*. In her book, she used a beautiful analogy for her experience of time. In my translation of the following passage, she referred to two cities in the Netherlands that are located about 11 miles apart:

> The idea of linear time has definitively been broken . . . It's a bit like the difference between driving a car or sitting on an airplane. Driving in a car I can never see Haarlem and Amsterdam at the same time, but I can when looking out of an aircraft window. (Klein, 2006, p. 246)

——— I CAN BE WHEREVER I WANT TO BE ———

Split in Two Pieces

Mohammad was taken to the hospital after a severe car accident, and there he "died." After quite a while, he realized that he must be dead. At that moment he thought of his mother, and immediately he found he was with her. Although the hospital was far away from the city where his mother lived, he could see both places at the same time. He could see how the doctors were working on him in the operating room as well as his mother preparing dinner. He said:

It was like I had split into two pieces, both with equal awareness. (*Mohammad Z NDE*, n.d.)

He also thought of friends and relatives, and the same thing happened. He could focus his attention on where they were without losing any sight of the operating room with the doctors and the kitchen with his mother. Then, finally, he left Earth as we know it and arrived in a wonderful and light environment where everything was perfect. As with many NDErs, he sensed that this was home. He said:

My presence on earth looked like a deportation to a strange and isolated island that was unpleasant and incompatible [with the wonderful and light environment]. Where I was now, there was no past or future, no close or far, no up or down, no dark or light, and all the relative things had lost their meaning. (*Mohammad Z NDE*, n.d.)

Here he saw other souls, some of whom were more advanced than he was, and some less advanced. However, there was no anxiety about this difference.

It was well understood that each of us are where we should be according to our own capacity and growth. (*Mohammad Z NDE*, n.d.)

On the Plane Together With Him

As Anita Moorjani (2012) described in her striking book *Dying to Be Me*, she had cancer and was dying in the hospital. Her husband and her mother sat by her bed, waiting for her final moment on Earth. Only one person was missing: her brother. He was on an airplane, on his way to Anita, hoping for one thing only: that he would arrive in time to see her alive. However, she was deep in coma with her organs shutting down, on the brink of death—the condition in which she had her NDE. During her NDE Anita noticed she could be wherever she wanted, because when she realized that her brother was not in the hospital, she was with him on the plane. There she saw him sitting with a worried face and she understood that he was on his way to see her. (Moorjani, 2012, p. 64)

Mother in the Railway Station

In 1969, an Indian homeopathic physician suffered an acute attack of dysentery and lost considerable blood. Suddenly he left his body and could see his body below. In that state, he was instantly aware of anything he thought about.

> In that out-of-body state I could fulfill all my desires as if I were Omnipotent, Omniscient! I thought of my mother, and I could see her running hectically on a platform of a Railway station hundreds of miles away! (*India physician NDE*, n.d.)

The mother later confirmed that after she had heard about the terrible situation her son was in, she had been desperately trying to buy a ticket for the train to the town where he was being treated.

Went to Her Workplace

Halil was walking to school to pick up his daughter when suddenly he had a heart attack. He collapsed on the ground. Someone was able to quickly call for an ambulance, and from only slightly above he could see everything happening. He saw how the paramedics put him in the ambulance and heard them discuss his chances of survival. They were pretty sure he was a goner. However, he himself felt perfectly well with no pain at all.

Then suddenly he thought of his wife and daughter and about how worried they would be when they heard that he'd had a heart attack.

> I knew that my wife's work was not too far, so I went to her workplace. I went to her office, but she wasn't there. I saw that her computer screen was on, and that she had been looking at an Istanbul real estate page with apartments and houses for sale. (*Halil T NDE*, n.d.)

Then the focus of his attention shifted. He realized that he had been able to go to his wife's office, and he became curious whether he could go to other places. He decided to fly upward. It worked. After a while he saw the whole town where he lived, and then he could see the coastline and all of Turkey. He didn't stop there. He could see the neighboring countries—and finally the whole world!

Then everything went black, and he started to be afraid.

> I . . . yelled, "Hello!" I didn't get a response. Then, I called out to a higher power, and suddenly, I saw immense light. I was able to float towards that light . . . which I believe may have been Muhammad . . . As I entered, I realized that I was getting sucked into some vortex. Then, I was in a cave or a tunnel. (*Halil T NDE*, n.d.)

At the end of the tunnel or cave he saw a door with "typical Islamic ornamentation." Before he was pulled back to Earth, he had a complete NDE. He had a life review, saw deceased relatives, and discussed the importance of his daughter keeping her faith. One moment he felt that things were changing. He couldn't move as easily as before. His weight seemed to have increased, and finally he understood that he wasn't allowed to enter a mosque, which his deceased relatives could enter. Suddenly he was back in his body.

It took him a while to cope with his experience and tell his wife about it. When he told her that he had visited her office and had seen her computer screen with the Istanbul real estate page, she confirmed that she had just been offered a job in Istanbul.

He is convinced that the experience was real. He said:

> The experience was timeless and vivid. . . . [The] experience was definitely real. It was 100% real, and nothing can change my mind. (*Halil T NDE*, n.d.)

———— DECEASED RELATIVES ————

After seeing a dim light, this NDEr went closer to it. The closer he got, the brighter the light became, and the more forceful the attraction. As with so many other NDErs, he said that he felt such a joy and peace. Then he saw other light beings, just like himself. And then finally:

> I was surrounded by my deceased relatives. I was feeling so much joy and lightness from seeing them. (*Arshan NDE*, 1996)

— EASY AND COMPLETE COMMUNICATION —

Telepathic . . .

Many NDErs have a conversation during their experience. This conversation can be with deceased relatives, with beings of light, or with the Light. In all cases, communication is described as particularly easy—not as it is on Earth, where words can get in the way. There, on the other side of life, the meaning of a message is always perfectly clear. This is because no words are used. It is a direct exchange of thoughts. NDErs often use the term "telepathy" to describe the communication.

> We talked telepathically—no words were needed. I heard the words in my mind. (Anonymous, 2013, April 17)

. . . and Overlapping

After having attended the funeral of a good friend, a man with a severe depression caused by seemingly drifting forever "from one job and living situation to another, never having any money (or a life)" took an overdose of pills and alcohol. The combination made him pass out, after which his NDE began. When he was moving towards the Light, he suddenly felt the presence of the recently deceased good friend. He then understood that he himself must be dead. About the conversation with this friend, he said:

> Our communication was telepathic and overlapping, so the answers already existed before the question could even be asked. It was as if our spirits were intertwined to the point that we were one and the same. . . . He seemed to be able to address an unlimited number of thoughts and feelings simultaneously. (Dale, 2008, p. 99)

The same friend also told the NDEr always to be aware and open to all messages that are sent to him. The reason is that even when our spirit is "trapped" in our earthly body, it is capable of picking up this kind of communication.

> I somehow knew this implied that I should encourage and appreciate time spent alone in order to be more sensitive and receptive to information being directed towards me. This information would ultimately serve to enrich and enhance my life on every level. (Dale, 2008, p. 102)

The deceased friend also discussed the Jungian concept of "meaningful coincidence"—synchronicity—with the NDEr and that this is not an empty concept.

Not Rich Enough

Orthopedic surgeon Mary Neal (2012) wrote an amazing book, *To Heaven and Back*, with her heart-pounding story about her kayaking vacation in Chile, where she had an accident and drowned. Then she had her NDE. In her book, she made it very clear that the world on the other side is completely different from our world.

According to NDErs, the other side is so extensive, so comprehensive, and all-encompassing, it is very difficult to put it into words. Neal explained this as follows:

> Our vocabulary is just not rich enough to describe the experience in a way that is understandable. (p. 73)

She met spiritual beings she knew and described it this way:

> Their presence engulfed all of my senses, as though I could see, hear, feel, smell, and taste them all at once. (p. 69)

Communication is always very efficient:

> We did not speak . . . but easily communicated in a very pure form. We simultaneously communicated our thoughts and emotions, and understood each other perfectly even though we did not use language. (pp. 69–70)

She said that what she experienced in her NDE was much more complete than what we experience every day here on Earth:

> I feel as though I am trying to describe a three-dimensional experience while living in a two-dimensional world. (p. 71)

Interestingly, in that other world she was accompanied by spiritual companions and saw beautiful buildings and large luminous halls while, at the same time, she also saw her physical body lying on the riverbank after she had been rescued by her fellow kayakers:

> As I was drinking in the beauty and rejoicing with my companions, I glimpsed back at the scene on the riverbank. (p. 72)

After she was rescued, many extraordinary and mysterious events occurred before she finally made it back to the US. Although those events were not part of her NDE, they still make for a great read.

— ALL KNOWLEDGE IS READILY AVAILABLE —

Know About Everything

I feel that we are limited here, and over there, things were so much clearer; there was just an instantaneous knowing about everything. Feelings were much more intense, and my conscious awareness could go anywhere in an instant. (Anonymous, 2018, May 14)

All Questions Answered

I felt as if all the questions I had ever wanted to ask, were answered simultaneously. It wasn't like I knew any one specific answer, more like I just knew everything there was to know, ever. I also had the feeling that as I received this knowledge from the beings of light,

I in turn gave to them all the unique experiences that I had accumulated from my time alive on earth. They gave me what they had, and I gave them what I had to contribute. It was very pleasing to do this exchange. I felt completely free and content. (Anonymous, 2003, November 11, 4:39 PM)

All Knowledge Was There

Rene Jorgensen had been pulled out of his body, and in his book he described his true nature:

What I experienced was my true nature as absolute and unbound consciousness. In this state there was nothing that I did not know—all knowledge was there. (Jorgensen, 2007, p. 6)

I Understood It All

In her book about her NDE, Deirdre DeWitt Maltby wrote how suddenly she understood

the complexity of life, of Source, of God. My soul felt I was now merging in unison with the universe. I was held in the palm of the force that created me, I was experiencing the Source! . . .

I could then see into eternity, see the entire universe. The past, present, and future all were one. I could feel the essence of every soul that had ever existed, or ever would. I was a million miles away from any earthly home I had ever known. *Yet this was home!*'

She understood that all knowledge is there for each one of us to understand to the same degree.

I understood it *All*. I was connected to it *All*, while *self* was still completely intact. (Maltby, 2012, pp. 48–49)

Answered Instantly

After realizing that she had been fatally struck by lightning, Elizabeth Krohn (Krohn & Kripal, 2018) saw a beautiful light that she must follow. Inexplicably she arrived in a beautiful garden in a heavenly setting. She immediately understood that time followed a different pattern. It was not linear, as she had always found it to be. She said:

> Things were happening in my field of vision and new capacities were awakening within me, but they were all taking place at the same time, all at once. (p. 23)

There she had extensive conversations with someone who spoke in the voice of her beloved grandfather, including the French accent. Yet she says that she does not believe it was her grandfather but, rather, that it was God who used her grandfather's voice to reassure her. She didn't want to look at the person sitting next to her in that beautiful, heavenly garden, because she knew it would be too overwhelming for her. She thought it was sufficient to just feel the presence of the unconditional love that emanated from that person.

The conversations with that person gave her a broad insight into, for instance, her private life and how time works. Her description of the way in which those answers came to her is reminiscent of other NDErs' descriptions:

> My questions were answered instantly. As quickly as I could conceive the questions, I received the answers. (p. 28)

She had the feeling that her stay in that beautiful garden had lasted two weeks, while on Earth she had been unconscious for only a few minutes. The special thing about the two-week conversation in that garden was that as soon as answers came, time seemed to become linear again. She said about this phenomenon:

> I have come to understand that this happened not because
> time actually became linear for two weeks, but because I
> would have no other way of "decoding" the information
> I received in the Garden here in this world. (p. 29)

Chemicals and Physics

In the middle of the night, Mohammad was driving towards his hometown of Isfahan, Iran, when he had a head-on collision with another car. He was seriously injured. Fortunately, a few minutes later a passenger bus was passing by and took him to a nearby hospital. There doctors and nurses began immediately to work on him. At first, he remained conscious. His mind continuously shifted from the pain and the anger about his situation to the young woman who had entered the room previously.

At one point he detected a shift. His anger and pain were gone. Instead, there was a deep feeling of tranquility. He also noticed that everything changed. His perception of things changed. When he looked at an object, he could understand everything about it:

> I could even understand the chemical compositions of
> objects I looked at and all its physical and mathematical
> properties. (*Mohammad Z NDE*, n.d.)

His perception of the young nurse was different as well. He could see "360 degrees around her, like I have totally engulfed her." He could also dive into her thoughts. She was feeling sad about his serious injuries. He wanted to console her:

I tried to tap on the shoulder of the young woman to get her attention, but my hand simply went through her body without any resistance. (*Mohammad Z NDE*, n.d.)

Similar to Mohammad's report, another NDEr reported:

I understood everything. Creation, purpose, love. Physics, numbers, existence. (Anonymous [Rachel Finch], 2019, June 10)

IT IS RIGHT IN OUR FACE

As a result of a ruptured ectopic pregnancy, a young woman had a complete NDE in which she got to understand everything. She understood that everything was actually very simple. It was so simple that she found it shocking that she hadn't understood while on Earth. She realized that when she was on Earth, she had forgotten everything.

As I waited, I remembered what I had forgotten, which was everything. I was astonished at the simplicity of why, what, who, where—all of it. I knew it all. I remember thinking that it is so weird that we don't remember any of it on the other side. It's so apparent, yet we cannot see it while living in the human form. At that very moment I likened it to an ant that could never perceive a human in its entirety, its complexity, or its completeness, yet we are right there to be seen if only the ant had the capacity. (Anonymous, 2009, April 18)

When she was told she had to return to Earth, she knew she couldn't take any of that knowledge with her. So, what it is really like and how simple it actually is, remains unclear to her. Again she is like a little ant that cannot see the reality that is clearly so obvious.

OUR FLESH IS LIKE A TV SET

This NDE is from a Chinese woman (*Chen M NDE*, n.d.; *Xue-Mei C NDE*, n.d.) who was an active member in the communist party. Her NDE happened in a hospital because she was allergic to the penicillin she received through an IV drip. Her NDE started in the customary manner, traveling uncontrollably fast through a tunnel. She was scared and screamed frantically. Finally, she exited the tunnel and arrived "in a bright, warm, and pure world."

She understood that her body was separated from her consciousness. She also knew that it was not a dream. What she said about that other world is:

> Your mind (soul) is existing and thinking obviously, but you are separated from the physical world without [having any possibility of] communication [with the physical world]. It is like a glass-door partition between you and the world; you can see everything of the physical world, however people on the other side can't feel your existence. (*Xue-Mei C NDE*, n.d.)

She also said, "I felt that several different dimensions coexisted," and "I existed in several dimensions." About consciousness she said that it still exists even when our body dies. She compared our physical body to a TV set:

> Our flesh is like a TV set and our consciousness is the signal. The signal still exists even when the TV set is broken. The consciousness of human beings is a kind of energy and it will never diminish. (*Chen M NDE*, n.d.)

This latter statement is comparable to a theory that the renown Dutch NDE researcher Pim van Lommel (2011) has proposed in his book, *Consciousness Beyond Life*: The body and brain can be compared to a radio or TV receiver that receives signals from the real program which takes place in a studio. The orchestra or the band is not in the radio or TV; it is in the studio. The orchestra or the band will continue to exist even if the radio or the TV breaks down.

——WE SHAPE OUR OWN EXPERIENCE——

Unearthly Landscape

In her impressive book on her NDE, *Awakenings From the Light*, Nancy Rynes (2015) described both of her NDEs. The first one was when she was run over by an SUV; the second one was three days later during the operation to reconstruct her spine. She wrote:

> The beauty and utter peace of the Place defies human words. I felt totally calm, loved, and whole. I also felt a deep, profound sense of LOVE permeating everything there. It was big love, as if the structure of this place was somehow made of love. Love was everywhere because there was nowhere that wasn't love. I can't explain it any further than that. (*Nancy R NDE*, n.d.)

She went on to say:

> The landscape continued to amaze me. Colors vibrated in harmony with different emotions. Trees weren't necessarily green nor was the sky always blue. They hummed with an inner energy and colors that radiated love, gratitude, and joy. Sometimes the trees would open up, and I saw distant, low mountains shimmering on the horizon.

Mists shrouded their flanks, and like everything else, they too seemed to radiate a deep, internal energy . . . Spirit wanted me to feel safe and comfortable here, so I was surrounded by a landscape that would seem familiar to me. Somehow my individual thoughts and feelings helped to shape the things I saw and how I experienced them . . . It seemed as though this place was, in part, a participatory experience. (Rynes, 2015, p. 31)

Park-Like Setting

Ellyn Dye described how she was able to change the setting she was in:

I realized I wanted more of a feeling of "place," because it was starting to feel disconcerting to just continue to float in nothingness, even though that nothingness FELT like a giant embrace by unconditional love and joy! As soon as I had that thought, everything shimmered and shifted, and I found myself looking out over a park-like setting. It was as if a giant hand with many paint brushes moved across the canvas, painting the scene with the greenest grass I have ever seen, the largest and most beautiful and most alive flowers and trees, rolling hills with pathways, and blue skies with birds overhead. The colors were brighter and deeper and more alive than any I had ever seen. I smelled roses, and sunshine, and freshness. The trees and birds and flowers and grass were alive and conscious, too. (Dye, 2023)

———— MANY RELIGIOUS FIGURES ————

In her book *A Passage to Eternity*, Azmina Suleman (2004) wrote in detail about her amazing NDE. At one point she described having met many important religious figures:

Then, from within that solitary ray of brilliance, I saw several of God's Messengers manifest themselves and stand before me in all their shining glory. . . . The individuals within this present group seemed totally immersed and enshrouded in light. They seemed to be projecting themselves out of a single ray of light as opposed to a series of separate and distinct lights, suggesting a lesser degree of separation from that one light Source, God. (pp. 60)

Although Azmina is a Muslim, the religious figures she saw were not only from her own religion of Islam but also from four other major religions. Some of them she didn't know, and only *after* her experience did she discover who the religious figures were. She saw prophet Noah, Moses, Jesus Christ, Buddha, Lord Vishnu and his avatar Krishna, prophet Mohammad and Lord Ali, and the Virgin Mary—or Bibi Miriam as she is called in Islam.

I recognized that I had, indeed, stood in the presence of true greatness. I sensed how all the illuminated Messengers of God that had stood before me were, in actual fact, different manifestations of the same Light. . . . I realized that they were, in fact, some of the most revered teachers of our times. They had brought a basic understanding of right and wrong, together with an understanding of ethics and morality to the people according to the comprehension of their times. They had also helped to raise consciousness of the one God amongst all peoples of the earth, and through different dialects had brought a clear awareness of the eternal kingdom of God. (pp. 62–63)

It is common for important religious personalities to be seen in NDEs, but usually NDErs see only the religious personalities

66

of their own religion. This NDE is unique in the sense that the experiencer got to see religious figures of no fewer than five major religions.

I AM THE ORIGINAL

The unexpected and sudden suicide of Rosemary's Thornton's husband had turned her world upside down. It took a toll on her health, and within two years she was diagnosed with cancer. On one occasion when she was in hospital, a minor medical procedure went wrong, and she bled to death, leaving her body more than 10 minutes without a heartbeat. In her 2022 book, Rosemary recounted what she had experienced during her NDE.

She found herself in a comforting blackness that was perfect. It was what she described as a comforting, velvety blackness, with "perfect peace times a million" as she said during one of her interviews, and she felt great. She realized that she had no heartbeat, and therefore she must be dead. She was intrigued by the whole situation. She even had to giggle. Then she felt a massive spiritual being next to or a bit behind her. It was "massive and powerful and gentle and tender." She turned her head to the left and looked up, which she found funny because she realized that being dead, she didn't have a head.

She asked, "And who are you?" The answer came back immediately, "You are the image and likeness, I am the Original" (p. 16). This answer amazed her, because she had studied the Bible throughout her life and in particular the text of Genesis 1:26, which was one of her favorite verses. And here was this presence that used this same text: that God created humans in his own image.

CHAPTER 4

Love, Unconditional Love

By far, the most important aspect of NDEs is love. But let me tell you now that the deepest interconnectedness with everything and everyone belongs to the other major aspect; more about that in Chapter 9.

The love experienced in most NDEs is completely overwhelming and thoroughly changes the NDEr after their experience. A very important aspect of that love is that it is unconditional. This quality is stated over and over again, in almost all NDEs, so it must be essential.

Try to realize what unconditional love means. It is love that is there without any preconditions. It is freely available, and you don't need to do anything in particular to receive it. There is no dress code: You don't have to be dressed in black or orange or any other color; there is no need for scarves, turbans, or other frills. You don't need to wear your hair in a particular style. You can be bald or have sidelocks. You may have a beard. You don't have to refrain from eating particular foods; there are no dietary restrictions. Shrimp is acceptable, as is pork or beef, and should you choose to limit yourself to eating only vegetarian or vegan, that's fine too. There is no obligation to pray five times in a specific direction, or to go to church, the mosque, or the temple. It is even alright if you don't pray at all.

This unconditional love is not withheld even if you admit to having caused harm to others or having done terrible things. There simply are no conditions to receiving this love.

You can just be who you are; being who you are suffices. This love is truly unconditional.

Mind you, not only is love on the *other* side of life paramount, but love on *our* side of life is paramount, too. The importance of *giving love* here in our world can be understood from life reviews (Chapter 6) and from what our purpose is on Earth (Chapter 10).

—1%, THOUSAND TIMES, EXPONENTIALLY—

When I would add all the love I had received throughout my life together, it would still be less than 1 percent of what I felt there. (Coppes, 2011, p. 36)

Stronger Than Anything

Rene Jorgensen was pulled out of his body. In his book he describes this sensation as being "overwhelmingly powerful." He bathed in "the transparent light of something so powerful, so indescribable, all words fade and disappear." Then he gave the following description:

It was love. I melted together with a feeling of love a hundred or maybe a thousand times stronger than anything I have ever felt in this dimension: "This is truth—this is what it is!" In that moment I knew the universe, "This is who I am—this is all there is!" . . . It was as if I had come home to my self—home to the ultimate nature of reality—home to love. It was all love. As I consumed all the love gathered from all the stars in the universe, I broke out in awe, "Wow! I did not know!" (Jorgensen, 2007, p. 6)

No Better Love

After having left his body, Dannion Brinkley raced down the tunnel towards a Light. The closer he got, the more love he felt.

He described this love as encompassing "all of the meanings of the world. It was as though I were seeing a lover, mother, and best friend, multiplied a thousandfold" (Brinkley, 1994, p. 8).

Then he met a Being of Lightand said about the encounter that "no one could love me better, no one could have more empathy, sympathy, encouragement, and nonjudgmental compassion for me than this Being" (Brinkley, 1994, p. 8).

Beyond Description

The only human emotion I could feel was pure, unrelenting, unconditional love. Take the unconditional love a mother has for a child and amplify it a thousand-fold, then multiply exponentially. The result of your equation would be as a grain of sand is to all the beaches in the world. So, too, is the comparison between the love we experience on earth to what I felt during my experience. This love is so strong that words like "love" make the description seem obscene. It was the most powerful and compelling feeling. But it was so much more. (Anonymous, 2011, May 11)

WORDS ARE NOT ENOUGH

Purest Love There Is

Rachel Finch (Anonymous, 2019, June 10) saw a pinpoint of light in the distance and felt the need to go to it. She said the desire to go there was like "remembering." Once she reached it and burst into it, she had the most wonderful feeling that she described as follows:

It was every incredible feeling that I will never be able to describe. It was immediate peace. Absolute, whole peace, all throughout me. There was no pain, there was no fear, there was no shame. I felt completely accepted. Totally whole and loved. Loved beyond comprehension.

Loved in my entirety. Loved with a Love I have not felt here. Loved with the purest love there can be.

Later, when the moment came that she had to return to Earth, she asked for one more moment to experience this wonderful feeling.

> . . . I was granted it. I soaked all the love I could into my entire being. It felt glorious. I felt pure and light and whole and loved and loved and loved. In this "moment," I understood everything. Creation, purpose, love. Physics, numbers, existence. I was completely at One with all of existence.

A Whisper

Deirdre DeWitt Maltby (2012) wrote how she was amazed by the greatness and perfection of what she described as unconditional love:

> The most awesome fact was that at the core of this feeling, knowing, and understanding was a great *Love.* Greater, brighter than the heat of a million suns was the magnitude of its being—Amazing!. . . .
>
> I was seeing the beauty of my soul; I saw the beauty of all human souls. Lost was any notion of myself as unloved or less than perfect. . . .
>
> There was also an understanding that this ultimate love being given to me came without judgment of any kind. It didn't matter what I had ever done, said, or been in the earthly world. I was still worthy of this indescribable love. Love is the Creator's gift to me. I became aware that we, as humans who are so far away from the light of perfection, are still loved. . . . (p. 51)

This realm beyond *is* nothing but . . . LOVE. Even the word *Love* is but a whisper of whatever the word might be that would describe what truly exists. There was no anger or hatred or criticizing. There were none of those other emotions that we use in conflict on this earth. They do not exist in *Love*. (p. 60)

A Sliver

The feeling of love was indescribable. I was consumed by it. It's like the amount of love we are able to experience within these mortal bodies can only hold a sliver of what we feel there. (Anonymous, 2021, January 28)

Unlike Anything Else

In my unpublished interview with Bill Gladstone about his NDE, he told me:

There was a unique feeling of bliss. I felt bathed in light, and deep unconditional love surrounding me.

The level of unconditional love was beyond description. It was unlike any experience of love previously experienced, even deeper than the love I remember from my mother who cherished me as an infant.

The Best Lobster

A student from a graduate school who had an NDE due to a heart rhythm disorder tried to explain in very lively terms how incredibly big the love was that he felt on the other side.

About the best way to describe it is to take the best steak, the best lobster, the most spectacular view, the best booze, and the most exquisite sex with the most exquisite partner. In other words, take the best you have ever felt, done, been, however, any way, anyhow and

73

take them all and throw them at you at once and it is just a small fraction of how delicious the feeling is. (Anonymous, 2006, January 30)

NONJUDGMENTAL

Undiscriminating

During her NDE, when Anita Moorjani (2012) was detached from her surroundings and the people she loved, she was surrounded by unconditional love. It "wrapped itself tightly" around her. She says that the term "unconditional love" is quite inadequate to convey the real feeling, partly because the word "unconditional" has been overused, causing it to lose its meaning. She said she never had known such pure unconditional love before:

> Unqualified and nonjudgmental . . . it was totally undiscriminating, as if I didn't have to do anything to deserve it, nor did I need to prove myself to earn it. (p. 66)

Later she said that the same unconditional love is not only outside us but is also within us. That is because we are part of the Whole, of the unity that is everything, and to which we all belong (see Chapter 9). She called it her biggest revelation:

> We are pure love—every single one of us. How can we not be, if we come from the Whole and return to it? I knew that realizing this meant never being afraid of who we are. Therefore, being love and being our true self is one and the same thing! . . . If we're all One, all facets of the same Whole, which is unconditional love, then of course who we are is love! (p. 76)

That is why she is convinced that she knows what our purpose on Earth is: "to be our self, live our truth, and be the love that we are."

What she means with "be our self" is that we must be our true nature. Our true nature is our core, the Love, the Unconditional Love that is within each of us, without any exception. When she realized that, she was told:

> Now that you know the truth of who you really are, go
> back and live your life fearlessly! (p. 76)

Overwhelming

Sandra Rogers (1995) had tried to take her own life with a pistol by shooting herself in the heart. She did so because she couldn't cope with life any longer. She hated it. In the life review during her NDE, she relived all the pain once more. It was a long, sad list of events, and I can only be amazed and astonished as to what a person can endure. She had had a disturbing childhood with arguing parents. After her parents' divorce, she and her mother lived in poverty, with a period that included an ongoing threat for custodial outplacement. She had troubled relationships with men, and by the age of 25 she had already been married and divorced three times. Being raped was a recurring theme in her life. She had been hospitalized many times for drugs overdoses. And please note that I haven't mentioned half of the traumas she endured.

The bullet missed her heart, and then she had her NDE. In it she met a "brilliant, wonderfully warm and loving Light." She and the Light looked at her life together. She said:

> I was aware as I relived each of these terribly painful
> events in my life that the Light, which was with me as I
> watched, felt all of my pain and sorrow and never judged

me, but instead understood and loved me. The love I felt
from the Light was overwhelming, and I never wanted
to leave it. (p. 70)

She was given the choice to stay with the Light or to return to
Earth. If she decided to stay, she would have to go back later,
to the "physical world and experience [again] all that brought
[her] to the point of shooting [her]self" (p. 11). However, if
she decided to return, she could continue to learn the lessons
from her current life. She would be allowed to take some of
the knowledge she gained during her NDE with her, but not
all. She chose the latter, and because of that she miraculously
survived her suicide attempt.

She has written a beautiful book about her experience,
Lessons From the Light (1995). In it, she described her experience briefly. The most important part of her book is about
the interesting views she was given during her NDE, for
example about anger, hate, love, free will, God, religion, and
sin.

ONLY LOVE

Everything Consists of Love

A 14-year-old boy had been bullied for seven years. It was
also the circumstance of his NDE. While he was at a camp
organized by his church, he was bullied again and sustained
severe head injuries. When he lost consciousness, his NDE
started. It was a deep NDE with an interactive review of his
own life, in which he could feel everything from the perspective of the people who had been around him (see Chapter 6
on life reviews).

During his experience he felt the presence of other souls,
had nonverbal conversations with them, went on a tour

through the universe, saw the most vivid colors, and heard the most wonderful music. He said:

> I felt connection to everything, all at once. There was no sense of separation, no division between here and there, between me and other beings . . . I felt the comfort and overwhelming love of others all around me. Love was what everything was made of, came from, and returned to. All-encompassing, unconditional love. It enveloped me like a warm blanket on a chilly day, and I just wanted to stay inside that love for the rest of eternity. (Anonymous, 2018, July 14)

The Essence
Another NDEr declared:

> I learned that what people think of as God is the energy of love, which binds the universe together, all life, all physics. The energy of love is the essence of life. (Anonymous, 2010, December 20, 16:33)

There Is Only Love
In her book, Carol Lynn Vengroff (2012) wrote what she had understood in her NDE about love:

> The most powerful force in the universe is love. As the sacred emotion of God, love transcends all. It is our true state of being. There is only love. (p. 37)

The Love We Gave
> The big thing is always to seek knowledge and to love one another. That's the greatest thing of all. The only thing we can take with us is the love we have given away. (Cox-Chapman, 1995, p. 58)

Strong Motto

Juliet Nightingale (2006–2009), mentioned in Chapter 1, had two NDEs and several other spiritually transformative experiences. Following her NDEs she had a strong motto which she dearly believed in:

"Only Love Prevails."

CHAPTER 5

The Light

The Light: Near-death experiencers say that it is overwhelming. It is breathtaking. It is comforting. It is pure love, pure peace, pure perfection. It is brilliant. It is like the sun, but much brighter, and it does not hurt the eyes. It is forgiving. It is irresistible. It attracts you like a magnet. Getting into that Light is like coming home. It loves you unconditionally. It accepts you completely.

That is a mere summary of something ineffable and indescribable.

 GIGANTIC

This Light Was Alive

Three boys aged 8, 9, and 10 years old, went for a walk along a river in Brazil. Their dad had told them not to go into the water, but at one point they did try to cross the river. All three were swept away by the fast current and drowned. One of the boys told his story, that he was taken by a beautiful angel into a bright light. He described it as follows:

> It was thousands of times brighter than the sun, and yet my eyes did not hurt. Somehow, I knew I was home. This light itself had a real feeling of love, like it was alive. I felt this love in my being (very hard to explain). (Anonymous, 2008, August 29)

He doesn't know how the three of them got back ashore again, but he remembers a beautiful dark-skinned man. He is certain it was the angel he had met during his NDE. Only after many decades did he ask his brothers what had happened then. To his great surprise, they told a similar story of drowning and being rescued by an angel.

Unstoppable Energy

One of Ponto3.org's interviews is with Geertrui Lagae (n.d.). She tried to answer the question what the Light is, but she found it difficult to put into words. Then she decided to say that you can't describe it as a feeling or emotion, but that it is a sensation

> that goes so deep, that is so beautiful, that is so . . . [she struggles to find the right words] it is a unity, it is all love. Yes, it's . . . energy, too, it's a kind of energy that you feel. And it's, you can't say, I'm going to stop that energy, I'm going to do something in that energy, that stops it, that doesn't exist there. It will last, it will remain.

Luminous and Golden

> The Light was brighter than hundreds of suns, but it did not hurt my eyes. I had never seen anything as luminous or as golden as this Light, and I immediately understood it was entirely composed of love, all directed at me . . . Though I had never seen God, I recognized this light as the Light of God. But even the word *God* seemed too small to describe the magnificence of that presence. I was with my Creator, in holy communication with that presence. The Light was directed at me and through me; it surrounded me and pierced me. (Sharp, 2003, p. 25)

All-Encompassing

Elizabeth Krohn (Krohn & Kripal, 2018) is sure that, in her NDE, the stunning beauty she witnessed and the way in which it was formed was there because it was tailor-made for her. She said that it was "her" heaven:

> I was surrounded by and suffused with an unutterable feeling of unconditional love. The love was all-encompassing and embraced me in every way: in the palpable scents that hung in the air around me like ornaments; in the soothing sound of the gently babbling brook nearby; in the cadence of the gorgeous otherworldly music surrounding me; in the visual floral feast before me; and in the deeply comforting knowledge that I was safe, protected, and unconditionally loved by God himself . . .
>
> It was a gift, tailored to me, from a higher being that loved me unconditionally. (pp. 25–26)

Gargantuan Energy Source

To get relief from her headaches, a young woman took too many pills and suddenly found herself flying toward the Light. Once in the Light, she understood that it is also a kind of entity. She had the feeling this entity was not human but, rather, "took a mild resemblance to a human" to make her feel at ease. She described this entity as

> a father, a god, a brother, a friend, a teacher, and most of all, an extremely superior entity that had total care for me, but seemed very strict with me at the same time, as if I was a child that he just caught running away with a cooky jar. (Anonymous, 2006, April 17)

She also said that the power of this entity was so enormous that she called it "a gargantuan energy source" and believed it was "God himself."

IN AND AROUND ME

It Absorbed Me

Rachel Finch reported that in her NDE:

I felt I was "home." I felt I knew this place/space/being. It was light. It filled every space of my 360-degree vision. It had no form that I can recall, which for a long time left me with other questions, but it was beautiful, and not blinding in the slightest.

It was as if I "merged" with the light. It absorbed me, I absorbed it, we became One, completely. In these moments, I learned much. About our existence as humans, about our planet and what we as a species need to do to resolve its problems, the healing that our planet and we as people need.

I was communicating with the light as well as experiencing being within it and One with it. (Anonymous, 2019, June 10)

I Became Part of It

At some point I met others, and we were in this dark void. Imagine you are wandering around in a large, dark room and meeting other people along the way, and we are all working together trying to find out what happened and why we are here . . . There was a light, some distance away, and I later found myself becoming part of it, but I very much wanted to figure out a way to bring the others with me as I was drifting away from them . . . In the light was this powerful feeling of love. I had come home and was appreciated here. It was such a strong thing . . . a feeling of love and complete acceptance towards me, in me, through me. I had come home . . . I very much wanted to go back and bring the others here. I

wish you could feel this . . . I can feel it all over again as
I write this, just pure LOVE! (Anonymous, 2018, May 14)

All Around Us

NDErs often say that the Light actually is always all around
us. Although we cannot see it, it is always everywhere. This
NDEr described it and then made a wonderful comparison to
convey its normality:

> The Light is all hidden knowledge revealed, all hurt
> healed, all longings granted, and an endless reser-
> voir of love, patience, humor, tenderness, power, and
> understanding . . . Like the fifteen pounds per square
> body inch of pressure that the atmosphere exerts upon
> us at sea level, its presence is so common and so con-
> stant we can't "see" it anymore. It "hides in plain sight."
> (Anonymous, 2015, April 25)

Be Gentle With Yourself

In her story about her contact with the Light, Lee Thornton
(2014) described it "as the essence of divine love" (p. 97).

Her contact with the Light was not superficial. On the
contrary, she even merged completely with the Light. This
merging is something mentioned by many other NDErs. Lee
put it this way:

> I was like an invisible, permeable membrane through
> which the Light passed and flowed, transforming me into
> the Light itself. It seemed to possess a universal spirit
> that was the consciousness and creative force behind
> human life . . . I felt no longer separate but enveloped by
> a feeling of unconditional love . . . The Light was both
> inside and around me. (p. 98)

She remembered her upbringing in which she had learned about the existence of "original sin." She also thought of her own sins and expected punishment. But the Light did not judge. When she was amazed about this, the Light said:

> My child, you mustn't take things so seriously. You are just part of an evolutionary chain, in which all life evolves at different stages of development. You are only human. You need not judge yourself so harshly. Be gentle with yourself. (pp. 98–99)

Melting Into It

Jang Jaswal (n.d.) from India had always thought of himself as being the center of attention, but during his NDE he was shown how insignificant he was considering the bigger picture of things. Then the Light shone on him.

> That was the best experience I had ever had in my life. The Light was of golden white color. It was more like . . . ah . . . I used to work in metallurgy at one time, and it was more like when the molten gold emits a kind of light. It is yellowish white light. It was that kind of a light. It wasn't hot or heat coming out of the Light. It was very soothing, very calm. When the Light was falling on me, at that time the wonderful thing happening to me was my brain or my mind stopped wondering all together. I was calm, peaceful. And there were no thoughts at all in my mind. No good thoughts, no bad thoughts, no nothing. I was just calm and at peace with myself. Soon after that, once the turbulence stopped in my mind, after that my whole existence, it started fading away. It was a kind of melting into the Light. And at that time this communication came to me, telling me that it's not your time. It is time for you to go back now.

Sparkled Through Me

Something went wrong in Catja de Rijk's (2021) cardiac catheterization, and she felt the strength drain from her body. An enormous calm came over her. Then her NDE started with a colorful tunnel. At the end of it she saw "the very beautiful bright white light." She said about it:

> I was drawn to it, I wanted to go there too. The white light sparkled through me [and soothed me] like water from a shower. So intense, so all-encompassing, that it's still hard for me to put it into words. The feeling is much greater than all the love I have ever experienced in my life. What I also found so special is that I had no difficulty looking into the white bright light. Whereas I put on sunglasses when the sun's light is too bright . . . As I write this, tears are running down my cheeks again. (p. 31)

Holographic Piece of It

In 1955, a few days before his high school graduation while attending a picnic with his classmates, Andy Petro went swimming in the ice-cold water of a lake and drowned. He sank to the bottom, and when he panicked, he heard a voice telling him to let go. When he did that, things changed. The pain was gone, and he felt a gentle silence. The blackness of the lake suddenly changed into the light of "a thousand exploding suns."

He wrote two insightful books about his experience (Petro, 2011, 2014). In the first one he told his story in a combination of prose and poetry—prosetry, as he calls it. In his second book he tried to capture his ineffable experience "in three-dimensional words." He tried to tell how it felt to be alive in the Light, which gave him very interesting insights. A few of the striking things he said about the Light:

The smallest piece of the Light, the building block of all that is, is a vibrating string of energy. And each vibrating string of energy is composed of, created from, the source of the universe of unconditional love. Unconditional love is all there is. There is nothing that is not unconditional love. Unconditional love is! (Petro, 2014, location 192–196)

When I was in the Light, I was aware of the existence of two of me—a three-dimensional, earth-bound me (earth-Andy), and a multi-dimensional, holographic piece of the Light me (Light-Andy). I am one and the same entity, existing in two different universes—one limited and the other unlimited. (Petro, 2014, location 66)

I knew I was a complete, holographic piece of the Light, and that there was no hierarchy between Light-Andy and the Light. (Petro, 2014, location 406)

Being alive in the Light is being in a happy place. The Light is permeated with joy, laughter, and humor . . . The Light is not a serious, somber, or stoic realm. The Light is void of fear, separation, judgment, condemnation, and terror. (Petro, 2014, location 487–491)

CHAPTER 6

The Life Review

During their NDEs, some people have a life review, and frequently this occurs in the presence of the Light. A life review comes in many forms. Some experiencers see their life as a film in fast-forward mode. Some see flashes or pictures. Some feel that these are memories of events. The overall feeling is described as "this is you." The smallest details are perfectly clear.

The life review is a refresher. NDErs say that they got to remember their place in the grand universal scheme and the purpose that they had on Earth—or, rather, that they still have, considering that all NDErs have returned to continue their earthly lives.

The life review also refreshed experiencers' memories in another way. It enabled them to be conscious of virtually all events of their lives and of the effect they had on others. This consciousness came in a very interesting way: They remembered these events not only as themselves but also as actually being the other people involved. In other words, they saw their own lives from both their own point of view and also from the viewpoint of everyone else. For instance, when they did something nice for someone else, they actually felt that person's happiness. This was not an experience of "*as if* they were the other person" but of "they *actually were* the other person." Likewise, when they harmed someone else, they felt that person's pain as that other person.

One woman once shared her candy with a school friend. It was right after World War II in the Netherlands, and candy back then was a rare luxury. During her life review, she felt the gratitude and happiness of her friend. Being her friend, she felt how thrilled her friend was to be considered worthy enough to receive that candy. She was surprised that the feeling of extreme happiness didn't stop with the friend but extended to everyone with whom the friend subsequently interacted, such as the friend's mother and, to her amazement, even beyond. In a very strange way, she felt that her kind gesture rippled further, to places she could not have previously imagined. This one kind gesture had a great effect on the world because it increased the total positive energy in it.

However, this NDEr also found out that a negative act makes the energy of the world shrink. Another one of her school friends was suffering from lice and asked her for help. She helped by offering to kill a few. The pitiful thing was that she didn't do it quietly. Instead, she made a big fuss out of it. By talking out loud about the lice, she exposed her friend. During her life review, she could feel the extent of her friend's embarrassment. She could feel the pain and suffering from this humiliation—as the friend herself. But worse than this painful feeling was the awareness that she had failed to seize the opportunity to add positive energy to the world.

She had the chance to bring love and warmth, but she didn't make the most of it. From her life review she understood that the goal—dead lice—was not important at all. Instead, the way she went about achieving this goal was important. She had chosen to make a great commotion, but she could also have chosen to work in silence. In that case, in addition to the dead lice there would have been something else: She would have comforted her friend and given her the feeling that she is appreciated, even with the little monsters crawling through her hair. Wasting that wonderful opportunity felt like an awful shame.

Reliving the event in her life review seemed not to be a matter of wrong or right but, rather, a matter of becoming thoroughly conscious of what had happened. She could reach this high level of consciousness because she was able to feel a very deep empathy, also towards herself. There was no punishment, although maybe the feeling of wasting a good opportunity was, in itself, a sort of punishment. But the word punishment still isn't right; NDErs describe it as a sort of deep regret, which they find most hurtful (Coppes, 2011, pp. 37–39).

———EVERY LITTLE DETAIL WAS THERE———

It Covered Everything

My life review was, well, lengthy, so I can't go into it here. Yet, it happened in less than a second and I saw EVERYTHING I ever did, said, wrote, thought . . . embarrassing. (Anonymous, 2006, January 30)

All Parts of My Life

I had an instantaneous flash of life review. It felt more spatial than sequential. The best way I can describe it is this: I've always been a pretty messy person. My life review took the form of a large disorganized room, and in that instant, I was able to see how all the parts of my life were connected to one another. I could see and feel how I had hurt people I cared about out of my own carelessness. (Anonymous, 2020, April 19)

Clear, Real, and Alive

While lying on the operating table in an Iranian city, Arshan had his NDE (*Arshan NDE*, 1996). He met deceased relatives, and after being surrounded by the Light he began to have his life review.

> My life and all of its events started to play in my mind, but it was very clear, real, and alive. It was like a slide-show, but I experienced all the feelings in these events again. Everything was shown in chronological order.

He mentioned that the whole performance, with all his life being displayed before him, took only a few minutes. After it was over, he assessed his life and what he had done. His conclusion was:

> I felt that overall, I was relatively kind to people.

EVERY CHOICE WE MAKE HAS ITS OWN REPERCUSSIONS

Options and Choices

A woman had a clear feeling that she was going to have a heart attack and was taken to a hospital. But from there she was referred to another hospital, and things went wrong in the ambulance. She felt how she was both inside and outside the ambulance. Then her NDE started, which included a life review.

She didn't really like going through it, but she knew there was no choice. It was a complete overview, from the first moment of her life until the last one right there in the ambulance. However, not everything was reviewed in detail. Only certain events were examined more closely. Those were the moments in which she had been cruel, such as at school when she had hurt another girl's feelings:

> When I reviewed that event, I felt her pain, knowing that God felt it also, and I knew I had an opportunity to

make a better choice but picked the group of girls over my soul. That was very awakening for me. I saw how I had harmed myself through poor choices that I had not realized were actual choices (at the time).

A big revelation to her was that everyone has all kinds of options and choices, but the one we choose to serve our highest good is also the one that will serve all souls to their highest good.

This was an opportunity to experience God from a whole new perspective, and that is what it is all about: perspective. (Anonymous, 2013, April 30)

I Felt the Repercussions

I saw my entry into the world, one childhood memory after another as distinct and as clear as if each were really happening. There was a doctor with a round mirror attached to his head on a band. I was jumping in my crib. Most things were pleasant to see, some things embarrassed me very much. In fact, revulsion and guilt took away any good feelings, making me so very sorry for certain things I had said or done. I hadn't just seen what I had done, but I felt and knew the repercussions of my actions. I felt the injury or pain of those who suffered because of my selfish or inappropriate behavior. (Anonymous, 2009, April 18)

—— WHAT I DO TO YOU, I DO TO MYSELF ——

Gone Against My True Nature

After René Jorgensen (2007) merged with the Light and understood that he himself is, in fact, pure love, he was given his life review. In his book he described it as getting to understand love. He also began to understand what was "not love." He realized that throughout his life he had lived contrary to his own nature, which was pure love. In his review he saw the people he had hurt during his time on Earth. He saw how he had hurt his mother when he shouted at her in anger. He saw a girlfriend he had cheated on and had not cared about her feelings. He also saw things he had forgotten, such as how he had teased a girl in the schoolyard in such a way that it had affected her all her life:

> She would be less outgoing and less able to love herself as an adult. I felt the full effects this would have on her family and the loved ones around her. (p. 7)

He was horrified because he saw how he had gone against the true nature of existence, which is infinite love, causing all that pain that he saw in his life review:

> The essence and purpose of life was love, but I had gone against love and therefore against my own true nature. It was as if I had been doing all this to myself—by hurting others I had hurt myself. We are all connected—we are all one. From the deepest part of my heart, I cried, "How could I do anything other than love?" (p. 7)

Then he saw all the pain and suffering in the world, all the poor people and people living in misery, all the conflicts and wars.

> We live in a world with so much agony, all against the nature of love. How could we accept all this? How could we live the way we do, not seeing the sorrow, not feeling the pain? (p. 7)

He decided to change his lifestyle and tried to devote his life to helping tormented people. Then the situation changed back to the feeling of love and bright light, and he saw a preview of his future:

> I saw myself loving people around me, having compassion for others, and devoting my life to helping the world. At the end of my life, I saw myself entering this light to return to where I came from. . . . (p. 7)

Ripple Effect

In her book, Carol Lynn Vengroff (2012) wrote about her life review, which was "crystal-clear" and "staggeringly detailed" about everything she had "ever felt, seen, touched, smelled, tasted, heard, sensed and done" (p. 13).

> What astounded me was that, simultaneously, I also experienced my life review from the vantage point of everyone and everything with which I had ever come into contact . . . I witnessed not only how my actions and deeds, but also how my thoughts and feelings had universal ripple effect! I was astonished!
>
> As I was re-living my *human* life, it occurred to me that my actions were not being assessed by anyone but me. I was not judged by a higher power. I was the only one who was my own judge and jury. (pp. 13–14)

She also said that God had always been with her at every moment of her life that she had just relived in her life review.

The Receiver

After Dannion Brinkley (2008) was struck by lightning, he died. While rushed off in an ambulance, he had his life review. He was appalled by what he saw. All the facets of his selfish and loveless actions were there in all their gruesome detail, and in his book, he called himself an "unpleasant" and "truly worthless person."

For instance, he relived the countless fist fights, not only as himself but also as his fighting partner, or what he calls "the receiver." He also felt what happened to the people he assassinated as part of his job for a secret American government agency—and, again, not only as himself, but also as the executed, as the "receiver." About his life review he said that the "depth of emotion" he relived was "astonishing" not only because of his own emotions but also because of the emotions of the people he met in his life and to whom he had caused grief.

There is more to say about this, because his emotions did not stop with himself or those directly involved. He also felt the emotions of the relatives and children of the people he had assassinated. They were the people who were indirectly involved, the people in the second order. They were people whom he had never met or had never even known existed. He said:

> I relived all of my kills . . . I saw myself make the kill, and then I felt its horrible results. (p. 16)

Finally, the emotions he felt were not only those of human but also those of animals. He gave two examples, one of a goat he had helped and the other of his dog he had reprimanded in a rough way (pp. 13–14).

Years later, when he had his second NDE, he had a second life review. Again, he relived the bad moments, but after his first NDE he had thoroughly changed his life. Therefore, his second life review also consisted of lots of wonderful moments where he had acted compassionately towards other people. For instance, he felt the joy with people from the hospices where he had volunteered, and lots of joy came from his many small and seemingly insignificant actions.

Humiliation

I was in a large theater, with a stage and velvet curtains on both sides. No one else was there. I was sitting in the middle of the row . . . and then one of my earliest child-hood friends came out onto the stage. She looked at me, and she let me know that she loved the games that we played and all the laughs that we had. Then it was my turn to tell her how I always had so much fun, but that I was sad when they moved away. We stayed there until we had exchanged love and admiration for each other.

Later, an older boy came out. He was the bus moni-tor. He conveyed to me that I had caused him humilia-tion. I listened to him. He used to bully my brother. So, one day I took his book bag and put it by the side of the house where the bus stop was. All the kids were playing. When the bus pulled up, the kids lined up and got on the bus. When it was his turn, he could not find his bag. He told the kids, "Not funny." They squeezed the window locks and pulled their windows down. I whispered to the others where his bag was, and they told him. Soon he was walking toward the bus and the kids were teasing him.

I had to go into his body and look at the kids hang-ing out the windows and feel the humiliation as he did. He had to go into mine and understand my experience. I had to send him love, and I told him that I was deeply sorry. He sent me loving kindness. When this exchange was over, we both felt understood and loved. I can't explain the depth of the healing. There were many more exchanges. (Anonymous, 2019, October 17)

Humbling

At a certain point, I was in this life and certain parts of it were being played for me, only I was re-living those moments, with complete clarity, both from my perspective and the perspective of anyone else involved. These were my words, my thoughts, my actions, all over again, but from every conceivable viewpoint at the same time. It was very humbling, and it's something I try to be mindful of today in my dealings with other people. Though when I think about it, it's so hard to push the ego aside and do the right thing, and I get the feeling that the next life review will be just as humbling or harder yet. I feel that we are limited here, and over there, things were so much clearer; there was just an instantaneous knowing about everything. (Anonymous, 2018, May 14)

Surrounded by Countless Movie-Like Screens

Andy Petro, who drowned during a picnic with his high school class, had his life review in a very special way. It felt like he was suspended in the center of a colossal, sphere-like sports arena or convention hall:

I was completely surrounded by countless movie-like screens—up, down, front, back, left, and right. Displayed on these screens were events from all of my lives, both here on earth and on other worlds. I was experiencing my life review. I saw, felt, tasted, smelled, and heard each experience. As I relived them, I relived each event as it was when it occurred . . . I could see and relive all my feelings, but most important, I felt the thoughts and feelings of all those I interacted with throughout my life review. (Locations 335–339 & 343)

I Felt the Pain Inside Myself

During his NDE, an Iranian man (*Mohammad Z NDE*, n.d.) met a very spiritual being. At first, Mohammad thought that it must be an important prophet, but after a while he was convinced that this being was much more than that. Apparently, it was his guide, who had been at his side all his life. He realized that everyone has a guide.

In the presence of this guide, he saw his life review. It was very comprehensive, and it started at the very beginning at his birth.

He said that before entering his mother's body, he felt that he was

> present in the entire universe, but somehow part of me focused away from this entirety and totality to move into the physical world and my mother's body.

He was not only the entire universe, but he felt a thorough interconnectedness with everything and everybody, something that many other NDErs have also said.

In his account he mentioned two events in his life review that made a big impression on him. Both were when he was a child. The first one was when he was fetching water. The bucket of water turned out to be too heavy for him. He decided to empty it partly near a tree that seemed to be thirsty. He said:

> I received such an applaud and joy for this simple act. . . .
> It was like all the spirits in the Universe were filled with
> joy. . . .

The important aspect of this act was that he had done it "purely from the heart."

The second event was less elevating. It was when he had beaten up a boy of his age. He saw the effects that this beating had on the boy, who was utterly unhappy and radiated negativity all around. Everyone, also the smallest animals such as flies, were affected by his pain. He also mentioned that even the stones where he walked felt the negativity. In fact, it spread over the world and all over the universe.

The interesting thing is that he saw that even the nonliving things, such as rocks on the side of the street, were affected. It also affected not only the boy's parents but also the boy himself throughout his life. It was like a ripple effect. His experience indicated that we all radiate energy, and that energy travels further than we think, just like the ripples in a pond in which we have tossed a stone.

He also said that inside himself, he could feel the pain he had caused the boy. That is, he was able to feel what he did to this boy as if he himself was that boy.

Even Animals: Guineapig

During her very deep NDE, Rachel Finch (Anonymous, 2019, June 10) had her life review.

> A "movie," for want of a better word, began to play. It was black and white and huge. As if I were staring at a giant screen that filled the whole of every which way I turned. The "movie" was my life from birth to death, every minute of it, every event I had ever experienced. I watched it and I relived it.

In her life there had been awful events that she had totally blocked from memory. However, during her NDE they were there, loud and clear. Nevertheless, she noticed that at these difficult moments she had not been alone. Her guide was always with her.

> I witnessed . . . the sexual abuse I experienced and suppressed as a young child, as well as out-of-body

experiences I had at this time and at night when I was lying in my bed. I could see myself flying out-of-body and I remembered. It was at this point I also saw and recalled a guide that had been with me throughout my growing.

Then she understood that she could feel what others felt as if she were those others. Interestingly, they were the feelings not only of humans but also of a guinea pig.

While watching/re-experiencing each moment, I found I was now able to experience each event through the emotions of all present at each time.

I watched my own poor mistakes and learned from every re-living. I watched myself as a child, bitten by a guineapigand in shock, half launch it onto the sofa. I felt shame at this time. Because I felt the fear of the guineapig. No one condemned me. I was asked only, what I had learnt. I was comforted at this time. Consoled and reassured. I had learnt so much. How big an impact my seemingly small actions had on a large scale. How my choices and behavior rippled through the lives of countless others. How the Love I showed spread like wildfire. How the way I mistreated others deeply hurt and affected them and also how that pain, fear, and confusion would then impact the lives of others, too. In the "time" I spent in this re-living, I developed a deep gratitude for many things. The experience of life for one. The people and the hearts that had touched my soul in beautiful ways and the fragility of being human.

—— NO ONE JUDGES YOU BUT YOU ——

Truth on the Table

Mally Cox-Chapman (1995) based her book *The Case for Heaven* on about 50 interviews with NDErs. With her permission, I have included three quotes from her book.

This NDEr had tried to commit suicide by inhaling deep gulps of water from the sea. He went through a tunnel and saw light at the end of it. He was judged by six judges and was given a life review. He said:

> The only thing that mattered was getting at the truth. Every thought, word, and deed that you've had comes into account. I mean that. I felt both accountable and forgiven. The judgement seems to be in part done by yourself. And the forgiveness, I mean what I understand to be the presence of God is total light and total love. There is no animosity there. In the presence of those judges I totally bared my soul. And when I was satisfied and they were satisfied that the truth had been told, then we saw eye to eye. (pp. 77–78)

The Judge Is You

As a swimming instructor at a Boy Scout camp, a 14-year-old boy initially had a distressing NDE, which fortunately turned into a blissful one (see Chapter 8). He saw his life review in the presence of what he believed to be an "angel." When it was over, he told the angel that he hoped he would not be judged too severely. The angel then answered that his life is evaluated by the most powerful judge. The boy asked when that would happen. The answer was:

> That has already happened. The judge is you. (Anonymous, 2004, March 4, 8:58 PM)

I Got a Thank You

During her NDE, Brigitte Buyle (n.d.) first went along an old staircase and then through a tunnel, and then she came to a door that opened for her. Behind it were a lot of people waiting for her. The welcome was overwhelming. However, in front of all those people she got to see her life review, with everything in it. She was ashamed:

> For all spectators! Can you imagine?

Then when it was over, she was surprised. The reason? All those spectators were grateful to her for all the experiences she had had on Earth.

> And what you got was a thank you for everything I had been through, for all my experiences. Everything. Everything was accepted, everything admitted, as if I was giving pearls, even the bad things, everything. You know, that was, yeah, it's indescribable. It is indescribable. And then I got a lot of love from them, all is well and thank you and we are very happy.

SMALL THINGS ALSO COUNT: IT'S ALL ABOUT LOVE

Small Things Have Great Impact

Irina was a primary school teacher. As she was cycling home, she was hit by a car. During her NDE, she was shown her life review. These were scenes from her childhood. She saw a girl whom her mother had told her to play with, but she didn't feel like it. She and the girl had a fight, and Irina ran home to get away from that girl. But the girl followed her and told Irina's mother that they had had a fight. Her mother forced Irina to say she was sorry. She did so reluctantly, and she kept her fingers crossed behind her back in such a way that her friend could see. During her NDE she saw the hurtful effect it had on the girl.

Then she saw other scenes from her childhood: images in which she saw what she had done to others. They were always negative images, never positive ones, although, of course, in her life positive events had been there, too. And each time the same feeling: Look what you have done to others. They were always small things which she had not considered at the time, but she understood that it was precisely those small things that could have a great impact on others. The point wasn't specifically what she had done; rather, it was that small things matter and that one must be more aware of them in life.

The images did not stop. Over and over again: "It hurt him or her," and continually she had that feeling that little things matter. She got the message. She wanted to get out of there. She was still confused. "I know now what it is all about," she thought—and suddenly her life review stopped.

> It is like having a hand in it yourself. As if you can decide for yourself what happens. (Coppes, 2020, p. 144)

She continued:

> There was a sense of acceptance. Everything I did was accepted. Everything was allowed to be. Everything was alright. There was a sense of unconditional love. You just feel it. From the inside. A feeling of coming home. It was the feeling I had when I had my first child. My child can do anything, but I will always love her. Such was the feeling. . . . (p. 144)

Here and Now

In my unpublished interview with Gayle Gladstone, she told me that she had her NDE as she drowned in Kauai's deep ocean on the high surf.

> I gazed at the beach and saw my nineteen-year-old daughter on the shore very, very small and far away. I couldn't make it in. I surrendered. I felt a great peace come over me. It was such a beautiful feeling. I thought WOW, I have done amazing things. I have helped others and stayed true to my life's mission "Helping others with loving kindness."
>
> I remember a sense of excitement to pass over. I allowed myself to go into death and willingly left my physical body. At that moment a bright light flashed in my presence, changing my consciousness, which altered my knowing.
>
> I found myself in a very large theater with myself sitting in the middle of the center row alone. It felt very important. I remember thinking "I am dry and this is not the ocean. This is an important place. Pay attention."
>
> This was a life review. I was on the movie screen. I liked my achievements I was viewing and was ready to meet my maker . . . thinking I had lived a good life and able to forgive myself for the mistakes that had come along with living and loving. I was content. My heart felt humble and my observations seemed to retain the innocence of a child.

Gayle felt content about life and how she had performed. But then her life review changed. She was shown the seemingly insignificant moments in her life when she could have made a difference in someone else's life—not by doing something big but by just paying attention to an unknown passerby, by saying or doing something nice, or by simply smiling. She said that the present is too important to be ignored. There is so much one can do in the present, in the now. Don't waste the opportunities at any given moment to create love.

Suddenly the film sped up. I was watching all these shorts of me in life. I remember wondering what is this? It was me crossing the street . . . me at the check out . . . me with other kids . . . etc.

Wow! This quickening of unimportant activity in my life review amazed me and made me think. Though I was feeling pretty good about my life, my unconscious behavior and the lack of opportunity I was allowing revealed how everything around me is an orchestration from the universe to help others, assist the collective evolution, raise its vibration, so I can know that I can help, too. It was shocking to watch. I had totally discounted the here and now. I had allowed my mind to take me away from the present. I was not paying attention . . . daydreaming and ignoring my physical life.

Once I understood that the present contained so many moments of love, need, and communication, the reel continued . . . all this happened quickly.

As I acknowledged my distraction and lack of attention in the present, I saw what happened or could have been avoided had I been paying attention . . . giving and being loved. There was an angry man I ignored or did not notice. What I was shown was he went home and beat his wife . . . An act of kind exchange or nod would have calmed the rage and avoided the incident. Another . . . had I just given a sincere smile the young woman would not have committed suicide. All was needed was a loving kind exchange to ground her and help her get back to center. There were rapes, bullying, and hatred that could have been avoided had I just paid attention to the energy and needs of others in my immediate surroundings. I recognized that by uniting our mind with our heart we are able to activate an automatic response of compassion to all energy around us. In this way we can share the one God-Love we are. I understood how our intention effortlessly creates a vibrational field which stretches out to those around us.

Have You Loved Others?

In his book *Return From Tomorrow*, physician George G. Ritchie (1978/2004) provided one of the first published NDE accounts. He had his NDE during a bout of double lobar pneumonia. He wrote about visiting hell (see Chapter 8), but also about having had a detailed life review. He said that

> everything that had ever happened to me was simply there, in full view, contemporary and current, all seemingly taking place at that moment. (pp. 49–50)

He saw himself as a tiny underweight, premature baby in in hospital, barely surviving; as a toddler playing with his sister who was just a few years older; as a teenager moving to a new house; and as an Eagle Scout. He saw his father introducing him to his stepmother, how he refused to love her. His exams, entering university, and hundreds and thousands of other scenes.

Then there was this question: "What did you do with your life?" It was a question about values, not facts. It was about what he had done with his allotted time, which was so precious.

To find an answer, his thoughts went to becoming an Eagle Scout. He was proud of it, but he understood that it was only something that gave him more esteem. And then he remembered how he had considered himself better than the kids who didn't go to church. He thought of how little he had achieved because he was still too young to have achieved anything. He thought of the insurance money that was due when he turned 70. And then the Presence beside him started to laugh a "holy laughter," without mockery. George understood from this that he was judging himself while the Presence beside him did not condemn him in the slightest. The question of what you have done with your life was implicitly there. George understood that it was related to love:

> How much have you loved with your life? Have you loved others as I am loving you? Totally? Unconditionally? (p. 54)

What You Do Out of Love

An eight-year-old boy drowned in a Brazilian river. During his NDE he had a life review. He wondered how bad an eight-year-old's actions could be. Then he saw how he had scratched the neighbor's car with a key. He felt the dismay of that man and assumed that he would be punished for it. But the angel who was with him laughed and said:

> Don't worry, that was just a lesson. It's the things that you do out of love that count. (Anonymous, 2008, August 29)

CHAPTER 7

Everyone Is Important

One of the first things I discovered when I delved into NDEs was that everyone is equally important. Homeless persons in our street or refugees in our wealthy country are no less important than company managers, religious leaders, kings, emperors, or presidents of our countries. The Light makes no distinction, which is because we all come from the Light and we all have the Light in us. Moreover, we all have an important task in life. Most importantly, the unconditional love on the other side of life is there for each of us. There is no exception; otherwise, it would not be unconditional.

WE WOULD NOT BE ON EARTH
IF WE DID NOT HAVE A PURPOSE

My Purpose

I saw that I had a purpose and that all beings have purpose. (*Yazmine S NDE*, n.d.)

God Depends on Us

I felt that everything was right—as it should be. There was a purpose to everything . . . I heard that God depended on us to work on earth. (Corcoran, 1996, p. 35; Dale, pp. 10–11)

I Wanted to Play My Part

I instantly knew how and why I wanted to impact the world. What part I wanted to play in giving to the world. Making my contribution. Leaving my mark. And the true motivations behind them. How I could. And why only I could in the way I could. Why those things are unique to me. And not for any of the reasons I might have guessed. I realized that within me there are reasons, and emotions, and motivations I had never before given myself credit for. (Anonymous, 2003, November 28, 10:36 AM)

Don't Waste Your Life

Yolaine Stout (n.d.) was raised Catholic, but when she was a teenager, she became an atheist. The reason was that the nuns at her school couldn't explain to her why children in Africa who didn't know Jesus had to go to purgatory or even to hell.

She married an Austrian man and went to live in Austria where she worked as an English teacher. However, it turned out not to be a happy marriage. She became seriously depressed, which exhausted her greatly. The straw that broke the camel's back was that it was determined that she couldn't get pregnant. She thought to herself, "Why live on if I can't be happy?"

She didn't want to commit suicide, because it seemed so bad for her parents, but she still wanted to die and preferably in a painless way. She had taken classes at the University of Innsbruck on autogenic training, which taught her how to gain a high level of control over one's own body. She thought that in that way she could slow down her heartbeat and eventually could make it stop.

Every night she did the exercises. At times she found herself in a kind of void-like situation where she couldn't feel her body anymore. That was not enough for her because she could still think and was therefore not dead.

One night, however, it worked. Suddenly it became very light in her bedroom.

It seemed like a thousand floodlights had suddenly come into the room. Everything was illuminated and crystal clear. I am very near sighted, and I need my glasses to really see, but then I could see down the hall, the pattern in the bed spread, and I looked out of the window and the sky was blue. I thought that I had just entered into a new kind of dimension. I moved to get up to explore this and as I was doing this, I heard 360-degree people talking. I realized that what I was hearing was every-body in that apartment building's dreaming. . . .

I shifted from wanting to die to wow . . . , it's another dimension. How exciting is that!

Then this other light enveloped me . . . Everything disappeared. It was like I had no body . . . there was a separation and a sense of self in it. But it felt like a warm bath of love. Pure unconditional love. All my worries, all my stress was gone. It was pure bliss. It was all light. I didn't see anything or anyone, but it was "home." I wanted to stay there forever. OMG this is love. . . .

Slowly it dissipated, it went away, and I was in my bedroom in a state of amazing awe. It was still lit up. I slowly turned to my side and I saw white robes standing next to my bed. I looked up. Holy moly. That's Jesus. He was looking at me with intense blue eyes. I had never seen anybody with such blue eyes. And he said to me one sentence. He didn't move his lips. I heard his voice in my head, or wherever I heard it.

"Don't waste your life thinking you're not loved."

And when he said the words "your life" . . . it was palpable how precious my life was, and not only how precious my life was but also how precious everybody's life was. Including that kid in Africa.

As Yolaine was an English teacher, she analyzed that one sentence over and over again. She said that the word "wasting" implied that there is life to be wasted. It meant that everyone has a purpose in life. A mission. There is a precious reason for being here, whatever that is.

> I understood that I had responsibility for my own happiness—that being depressed was "wasting" my life. I had to figure that out. I started to look for what my purpose in life is and how to overcome my depression. I had a choice. All the time there are choices.

In her beautiful presentation, Yolaine talked about her depression, which was not immediately over after her experience. It is very interesting to hear how she started to look at things differently and how, as a result, she eventually got through her depression and went on to live a life filled with meaning.

A Plan for My Life

A young boy was riding his bike and got hit by a car. He was hurried to hospital, and from above he witnessed the surgery required to keep him alive. Then he left the operating room and found himself surrounded by "darkness, nothingness, but fully enveloped in the peace and love of God's presence."

He had to go back again, meanwhile convinced of something very important:

> The most significant thing I take from this experience is the conviction that God exists, loves me, and has a purpose and plan for my life. (Anonymous, 2010, December 20, 16:48)

We Already Know Everything

In my interview of a man with the pseudonym Noël de Waele, he revealed that his NDE occurred while he was in a deep psychological crisis (Coppes, 2021/2022). Marital problems had had a serious impact on his life and health. He was terrified that his 12-year-old son Maurice would be taken from him. During his NDE, he received not only his late sister's encouragement to start living his life but also the message that Maurice would stay with him. He continued to remember other truths from his NDE, such as that all people matter. Everybody. Without exception. He said:

> You wouldn't be here on Earth if you weren't important. Because everyone is connected. This does not only apply to people but to everything alive on earth, the animals, and the whole of nature. We all have a mission, and that mission is to be happy and make others happy. We need to create a world we can all live in. A world we can share together. NDE messages have the potential to lift the world to a higher consciousness. (p. 25)

He also felt that the world is having a rough time.

> It's a mess. But if you don't go down, you can't go up. I have experienced it myself. The same applies to the world. A 'wake-up call' is needed before people realize that we need to change, not only on a personal level, but also on a global level. (p. 25)

Noël said that people's most important qualities are what he calls the "heart qualities." He named a few: love, compassion, friendship, peace, and cheerfulness.

If you can live from your heart, it is wonderful for yourself and others. Apart from love, forgiveness is the most
beautiful "heart quality." If you yourself are pure, you
can forgive your worst enemy. (p. 25)

When I asked how we can do this, he said:

We don't have to learn anything, because we already
know. All of it is within you. It's what you are born with.
(p. 25)

WE ARE DIVINE

Part of the Light
[I realized] that I was part of the Light, of God in general, like a grain of sand on the beach. I was a grain
that is God, but God itself was the whole beach. (Cox-
Chapman, 1995, p. 80)

Little Gods
We are all children of God, and therefore, we are little
Gods, too. We just have to remember our divinity. (Bur-
ton, 2002/2003, p. 14)

God Flows Through Us
God is not something outside of us. Far away, and
unknown. He flows through us as the Eternal Presence.
(Klein, 2006, p. 105)

Fragment of the God Force
After a hemorrhage during childbirth, a woman (Anonymous,
2017, February 17) had her first NDE, which was immediately followed by a second one when they gave her a transfusion with blood that was too cold. During her first NDE,

she shot into space and saw Earth from a great distance. She loved it and felt an enormous connection with our planet. This was followed by a life review, a tunnel, and a meeting with her deceased father, among others. She understood that free will is an enormous privilege:

We decide, and that has tremendous power.

During her second NDE she had an extensive exchange of information with a group of what she called "teachers." Although she could ask anything, she was unable to take much of the information with her.

Both NDEs have greatly changed her attitude toward life. She understood that we are here of our own free will to fulfill our task. She said it like this:

[The NDE] gave me direct experience of my life everlasting and it proved to me I am here by choice, to fulfill my Soul's purpose, that I am an individual and unique fragment of the God Force, and that I will never be seen again in all the worlds in this form. Therefore, I am precious, exceedingly precious. It does not matter what I do; I am asked only to be the love that I, and I alone, carry on this Earth now when I am so desperately needed.

I HAVE A GUIDE

Being out of his body after a severe car accident, Mohammad (*Mohammad Z NDE*, n.d.) had the feeling that he was not alone. He was important enough to have a guide who had been with him throughout his life.

Eventually, I noticed him. He was an amazing, divine human-like figure who radiated lots of love and light.

113

The NDEr then felt total love for this divine human-like figure and received unconditional love in return.

> First, I thought he must be a prophet or religious figure, but then I thought that he is even above all that. I realized that he has always been with me throughout my life, always. He was my guide.

And he then concluded that everyone has a guide, which implies that apparently everyone is important enough to have one.

BEING GAY IS OKAY

Liz Dale (2008) wrote a significant book with a compilation of 21 NDE stories from the gay community. This great book shows that gay people also have blissful NDEs in which they, too, are welcomed into the Light. It demonstrates that being gay is no issue at all for the world of Light. She provided more of this kind of evidence in her new book co-authored with Kevin Williams (2022).

In her compilation of NDE stories, two of particular importance stand out for this chapter. The first story is about Andre, a sound and light technician and rock & roll musician. He had his NDE associated with a ruptured appendix. During his life review he heard the words, "All human beings are good." He also understood that all people are connected—and that we always were and always will be. Then, once again, his life was reviewed:

> This time I could see all self-doubt that I had in my life centered around the question of my being any worth to God, since I was a gay man. It was then that I mustered up the courage to ask these beings something I could sense they were waiting for me to ask. I asked, *"Is it*

okay to be gay?" and they laughed and said, *"Who do you think made gay people?"* I remember us laughing for what seemed like 1000 years. (p. 32)

In the second story the NDEr had a telepathic communication with a good friend who had died only a few days before. This friend had become great and powerful and seemed to know about the NDEr's estrangement from family and friends. This was because the NDEr had very low self-esteem owing to his own disapproval of his sexual orientation. He said:

[The good friend] indicated most empathically that I should always openly celebrate and honor my sexuality as a precious gift from God. This was a startling revelation to me, especially after a lifetime of secrecy, fear, and guilt. (pp. 101–102)

In addition to the NDEs in Liz Dale's book, other NDEs can be found in which the experiencer discovers that on the other side of life there are no ill feelings whatsoever toward gay people. One such case (*Kerry B NDEs*, n.d.) is that of a woman who had an allergic reaction. She felt her throat closing, and she could not breathe.

Her wife begged the ambulance paramedics, who happened to be outside their flat, to come in and help. Meanwhile, the woman with the allergic reaction was having her NDE. She said:

[I] was sucked through the air by a powerful, yet gentle and loving force. It was like I was riding on a cosmic elevator.

Her fast ride was slowed down by her grandparents who unexpectedly emerged from the void to beg her forgiveness.

They now understood that being gay isn't easy, especially if you grew up in the strict religious Southern U.S. Bible Belt. The NDEr had lived in terrible fear for years and had been a victim of hate crimes, among other things.

It felt good that her grandparents recognized all of this, but she wanted to continue her hi-speed journey, because in the distance she saw the Light attracting her.

When she got there, she saw in awe that it was God. She received her life review, which included her lesbian feelings. She wondered how she could be with God because she had always been taught that God throws homosexuals into hell, as they are an abomination. With absolute humility she asked:

I'm gay, will you still love me?

In response, she was taken up in a loving Divine embrace and taken across the universe in a happy flight. Then God reaffirmed humorously, and with a Southern accent:

You are my child. I love you. I love you. I love you.

And then, "Go get 'em," as if God were a coach sending a player back onto the field. Soon after, she was back in her body. The nurses had managed to bring her back.

CHAPTER 8

Distressing NDEs

At the start of this chapter, it is extremely important to clarify a couple of things, both conclusions from research. First, it is wrong to think that fearful experiences only happen to "bad" people and heavenly experiences only to "good" people. Second, the terms "good" and "bad" don't apply on the other side of life. Those terms belong to our Earth and are created by humans to evaluate others or themselves.

There is a lot of information about blissful NDEs but much less about distressing NDEs. It took Bruce Greyson and Nancy Evans Bush nine years to find 50 people for a study of distressing cases. They analyzed their data and observed three distinct types of experiences. These three types are still used to categorize distressing NDEs.

1. The first type consists of experiences that are almost identical to the blissful ones, but instead of having wonderful feelings, the NDErs experience everything as horribly out of control.
2. The second type consists of experiences where the NDErs have the feeling that they are alone in a dark everlasting void where they are hyperaware of being eternally isolated.
3. The third type consists of experiences in which the NDErs find themselves in an outright unpleasant or even hellish environment (Greyson & Bush, 1992).

I would like to recommend several books that shed some light on distressing NDEs. They are *Blessing in Disguise* by family physician Barbara Rommer (2000), and two books by Nancy Evans Bush: *Dancing Past the Dark* (2012) and *Reckoning* (2021). Rommer suggested a fourth type of distressing experience in which the life review causes great distress to the NDEr. Bush nonetheless included in her first category these otherwise pleasant NDEs with a guilt-ridden life review.

Rommer (2000) interviewed more than 300 NDErs of which an undisclosed subset consisted of distressing NDEs. The interesting thing about Rommer's book is that she suggested that distressing experiences can be beneficial to the NDEr to expand their consciousness and to be open to higher truths. She cited changes in beliefs, behaviors, and values that have improved the NDEr's life. She also mentioned psychic and spiritual gifts that the NDEr derived from their experience (see also Chapter 12 on aftereffects). That is why she called these experiences blessings in disguise. However, such changes are also to be found among NDErs who had blissful experiences, and the question still remains why the experience had to be distressing.

Another important comment in Rommer's (2000) book is that a "mean" person need not necessarily have a frightening or hellish experience, nor would a gentle, kind person necessarily have a blissful one; Bush (2012, 2021) drew a similar conclusion. Rommer said that everyone could potentially have a distressing NDE. She also believed that negative programming during childhood, or a distressed or even a fearful mindset just prior to the experience, may contribute to an NDE being distressing. She also believed that the NDEr unconsciously determines the imagery that occurs in distressing NDEs. M. K. McDaniel (2020) drew the same conclusion based on her distressing NDE (see below in this chapter). I agree with Rommer and McDaniel and believe that to a certain extent, the content of an NDE is tailor-made to the experiencer (see also Chapter 3).

By comparison, Bush (2012, 2021) chose to stick to "just the facts" that she found in her extensive study of distressing NDEs. I would like to share five of them here.

By far the majority of reported NDEs are pleasant or better, but as many as one in five may produce one of the three types of distressing NDEs, with intense loneliness, panic, despair, guilt, or even sheer terror.

- As with blissful NDEs, distressing ones may happen to people from all walks of life.
- NDEs are not static and can switch "from unpleasant to pleasant or, less commonly, the other way around."
- Distressing experiences feel just as real as blissful ones.
- And, in my opinion, the most important fact—one that Rommer also concluded: There is no evidence that distressing experiences happen only to "bad people."

The concept of "bad people" is a difficult one, because it is colored by, for example, current morals or religion. We tend to think that "bad people" are those who hold inappropriate convictions or display unacceptable behavior, such as murder or suicide. But even "bad people" can have blissful NDEs. Dannion Brinkley (2008) is an example of what many people would call a "bad" person. He killed people but nevertheless had a blissful NDE. See his story further down in this chapter, where you can also find more on the peaceful and comforting deathbed visions of prisoners in the Angola Louisiana State Penitentiary. These cases serve as an additional indication that "bad" people can have blissful experiences when they die. Elsewhere in this book there are quotes from blissful NDEs by people who attempted suicide. Conversely, there are examples of "good" people who had a distressing experience, for example the 14-year-old boy (Anonymous, 2004, March 4, 8:58 PM) and M. K. McDaniel (2020), as discussed below.

One thing that I have learned from NDErs is that the notions of "good" and "bad" are earthly terms that have no meaning on the other side of life. Therefore, there must be another reason why distressing NDEs occur.

"BAD" BOYS FEEL BLISS

Entire Villages Destroyed

In his amazing book, *Saved by the Light*, Dannion Brinkley (2008) described his life review (see also Chapter 6). He described it as

> . . . not pleasant. From the moment it began until it ended, I was faced with the sickening reality that I had been an unpleasant person, someone who was self-centered and mean. (p. 9)

He summed up what he considered to be unpleasant. In his childhood he saw himself torturing other children, stealing their bikes, making their lives miserable, and engaging in countless fights. Later in life, he saw his involvement in a government agency in which he carried out executions of people abroad who were considered enemies of the U.S. government. Together with others he blew up a hotel with 50 people in it while aiming to kill only one official. He also added:

> While in action I had seen women and children murdered, entire villages destroyed, for no reasons or the wrong reasons. (p. 16)

During the life review in his NDE he felt the pain he had inflicted on others and saw the truth about himself, namely that he didn't care what other people felt. He thought of himself as a "truly worthless person" (p. 19).

Nevertheless, apart from the life review, which was absolutely dreadful, his NDE was a blissful one, in which he met a Being of Light that overpowered him with an abundance of Love.

> As I gazed at the Being of Light I felt as though he was touching me. From that contact I felt a love and joy that could only be compared to the nonjudgmental compassion that a grandfather has for a grandchild. (p. 24–25)

This NDE shows that "bad" people can have blissful NDEs.

Pleasurable Deathbed Visions for Crooks

A very interesting study by Marilyn A. Mendoza (n.d.) focused on the deathbed visions of prisoners with life sentences.

The Angola Louisiana State Penitentiary is a high security prison in the US for dangerous criminals who often serve a life sentence with no possibility of release. In other words, these prisoners are far from "little darlings." They are referred to by many others as "bad" people: murderers, rapists, drug traffickers, and armed robbers.

A life sentence generally means imprisonment until death, and as is the case outside prison, these convicts frequently die of terminal illnesses. Therefore, there is a hospice in the prison which, interestingly, is run by inmates themselves.

Interviews with these hospice employees showed that, over the years, 26 of the 29 employees had witnessed patients who had experienced deathbed visions. Only one of those many cases was a clearly distressing one. All the other cases had been pleasant, in which dying convicts had seen angels, beautiful gardens and gates, the Light, and deceased relatives who were ready to meet them and accompany them through their transition from this life to the next.

Mendoza (n.d.) concluded that pleasurable deathbed visions were as common among these serious criminals as among the rest of the American population. She found that 98% of the deathbed visions in her study were peaceful and comforting. Again, we see that "bad" people can have beautiful experiences. Of course, deathbed visions are not NDEs; unlike NDErs, deathbed experiencers usually remain conscious, don't usually report leaving their bodies, and proceed to die. Nevertheless, deathbed visions are closely related to NDEs; both experiences share many similar images of spiritual entities and environments and are usually profoundly pleasurable—whatever the experiencer's earthly deeds.

GOOD PEOPLE GET HELL

A 14-Year-Old Attacked by Evil Entities

In Chapter 1 I described the case of a boy who was at the dentist when things went totally wrong. He then had an enjoyable experience in the void. Below is an example of someone with a distressing NDE in the void.

This 14-year-old boy (Anonymous, 2004, March 4, 8:58 PM) worked as a swimming instructor at a Boy Scout camp. During a swimming lesson, one of the younger scouts had a panic attack. The young instructor jumped in to save the scout—initially successfully, because the young scout allowed himself to be dragged through the water to the shore. But suddenly the scout had another panic attack, thrashing around wildly, resulting in a sharp blow to the head of the instructor who then lost consciousness.

It's black. Pitch black. I see nothing. There is nothing. I strain to see something, anything. I don't like this. I'm scared. I feel I am in a universe devoid of all things. It is vast without end and completely and utterly empty. There is no one else, nothing else. I am alone. There is no person, no life, no death, no love, no hate, no salvation. There is only a vast emptiness except . . . for me. The loneliness overwhelms my senses. I would welcome anything. Please. Please. I can't stay here.

Then, suddenly, he saw something. He listened carefully and gazed into the darkness. He wondered if his mind was deceiving him. Then he heard laughter, but he did not know whether he liked the sound. It was more like someone laughing at him. Then he saw a very small speck of light that seemed to come closer as the laughter grew louder.

It can't be . . . it's a skull and it's laughing. It isn't a good laugh. It's sinister . . . It speaks and tells me I am there forever, with him. I begin to hear others talking. They are coming nearer with conspiratorial voices that are evil and menacing . . . I'm scared. I feel their presence, encircling me. These are creatures of the darkness . . . Ouch. Something clawed me and I am being bitten as if being tasted. Then, they are set loose upon me clawing, scratching and biting. It feels like my skin is being stripped off. God, please help me. The attacks continue. Then I recall an old parish priest told me that evil cannot remain in the presence of God. I call out, Lord, Jesus Christ, help me please. Help me. The attacks subside and soon stop altogether. The dark entities of evil slink away into the darkness. I am alone again in the black emptiness, but I am relieved.

It ended well because another speck of light was approaching. At first, he was afraid that the skull and those other evil entities had come back, but they were multicolored bubbles. And there was one in which he saw a guardian angel.

He spent many years reflecting on his distressing NDE, wondering again and again why a 14-year-old boy would have an experience involving an encounter with such evil creatures. He said:

> After all, how bad can a fourteen-year-old boy's life be that he should deserve such treatment?

He concluded that it was because it was not yet his time, and, therefore, no one from his already-deceased family or friends could have known that they should welcome him. He thought it made him easy prey for the "dark side entities."

An Ordinary Woman in Hell

M. K. McDaniel (2020) wrote an extensive book about her distressing NDE: *Misfit in Hell to Heaven Expat*. I think that she was very brave to write this very fascinating book. Including a description of her life before and after her NDE, her story shows that she is just an ordinary woman—certainly not someone you would expect to have a distressing NDE.

She was on a ventilator after lung failure and suddenly found herself in a hellish environment. She described it as including "scenes of epic destruction," "dark shapes dart[ing] crab-like among the smoldering ruins, hissing like snakes," and "has-been humans, mere skin and bones covered by rags" (pp. 313–314).

She was determined to get out of there and shouted that she would not give up. She described various frightening scenes. In one she was mercilessly ridiculed; in another she witnessed abortions being performed in an industrial way. She was attacked by a mob who told her that they had AIDS, and now she had it, too. Finally, she found herself being part of a group of miserable women who were about to be prostituted.

She asked the leader of the group, the "Madam," if this wasn't a very miserable day. The Madam replied that it was Christmas on Earth, which always was the saddest "time" in hell. This response inspired McDaniel to sing a religious Christmas carol, and the other women started to sing along. This enraged the Madam, but McDaniel closed her eyes and continued singing. The moment she was going to say the word "Jesus" in the song, she suddenly found herself in a place where she was "flooded with an abundance of love, peace, and joy!" (pp. 328, 331).

She made it to heaven.

Later, after she had returned to Earth and to her body, she struggled with what she had experienced. Certainly, they had not been hallucinations, because her experience had been more real than life.

After thinking for a long time about what she had gone through and, in a sense, confronting her distressing experience, she began to realize that the various components of her experience related to fears she had had and to painful experiences she had gone through in life. During the time she was trying to come to terms with her traumatic experience, she asked God what she should do to avoid hell, and over the course of months she heard several words that together formed the sentence she now carries as a mantra: "Be loving, kind, merciful, forgiving, encouraging, grateful, non-judgmental, and useful" (p. 461–463).

NO PUNISHMENT

In Western culture we tend to see distressing NDEs as punishments, but there is plenty of evidence to counter this assumption. I have already provided a few examples. The evidence shows that blissful NDEs can happen to what might be considered "bad" people and that distressing NDEs can happen to "good" people. That is why we must move away from an explanation in terms of guilt and punishment and look for a different explanation.

In her books, Nancy Evans Bush (2012, 2021) suggested that distressing experiences can arise from the collective unconscious. This term, coined by the Austrian psychiatrist C. G. Jung, refers to the unconscious mind populated by a multitude of instincts and archetypes. During their NDEs, people could be confronted with some of the unpleasant archetypical (universal human) images that arise from this collective pool. They are then left with an outright distressing NDE, or they may have a blissful NDE but see distressing scenes in which they themselves have no part.

The distressing images from this collective pool of instincts and archetypes could arise because the experiencer already has some feelings of guilt or unworthiness—or perhaps because of their upbringing, or a religious background that emphasized sin and punishment, or fear that activates distressing images from the collective unconscious. And perhaps distressing images pop up randomly.

Likewise, in blissful NDEs, the imagery could also be drawn from the same collective unconscious pool of instincts and archetypes. This idea is not so strange considering that the content of NDE stories differs greatly. The reason for this could very well be that to a certain extent our consciousness retrieves familiar images and thus colors the NDE—or at least the initial part. The coloring can go in several directions: blissful, frightening, or a mixture. Although NDEs unfold seemingly outside the control of the experiencer, NDErs sometimes appear to have a certain degree of influence over their experiences—as was illustrated by a few examples in Chapter 3. Thus, although experiencers may sometimes unwittingly "tap into" distressing aspects of the collective unconscious, they may also have the ability to change their distressing circumstances. This may especially be the case if their intention is directed at that which is benevolent and loving.

Therefore, in my opinion, we need to look through the imagery of both pleasurable and distressing NDEs and get down to the essence. And what is the nature of that essence? Evidence from NDEs indicates an unconditional love (see Chapter 4) and a profound interconnectedness (see Chapter 9).

In any case, we need to stop seeing the distressing NDE as a punishment for "bad" behavior. In the words of Nancy Evans Bush (2021), distressing NDEs should rather be understood as "developmental steps to be worked through en route to personal growth" (p. 117).

We need to try to understand where the distressing imagery comes from. Perhaps the question should be, "What caused this imagery?" Of course, this question applies equally to blissful NDEs. From this perspective, blissful NDEs, too, would be seen as the same developmental steps necessary for personal growth. To quote Bush (2016):

> No near-death or other spiritual experience is complete until it has been integrated—incorporated in a meaningful way into its owner's life and understanding. (Location 1497)

This integration process is hard work. Having an NDE is not easy, which applies to both blissful and distressing NDEs. But especially the NDEr with a distressing experience must confront it and try to figure out where the distressing images came from and how to use them to grow spiritually.

In any case, the message here is to move away from the explanation of guilt and punishment, because growing evidence indicates that this very human-moralistic explanation is incorrect.

FAR FROM PLEASANT

A Painful Life Review

Rene Jorgensen (2007) had a life review (see also Chapter 6 on life reviews), and he found it an extremely distressing event. As such it could be categorized as a Type 1 experience (see the explanation in the introduction of this chapter). He saw what he had done to others throughout his life on Earth. In addition, he had also seen all the agony, all the pain and suffering in the world, all the people living in poverty and misery, and all the conflicts and wars. He wrote,

> This was far too much for me to bear. My heart could not contain all the world's grief. In an extreme intense sensation, I felt my heart literally tear in two, and the pain was so strong I could not bear it. (p. 7)

Attempted Suicide

The first time this man had an NDE, it was a partial experience. It happened in the context of a motorcycle accident. He saw doctors trying to keep him alive. He saw no light but felt at peace, and then he lost his fear of death. Later in life, he had many issues in his family, including his divorce, and consequently losing his family. It took a huge toll on him. One night while he was drinking, he started to think about everything that had happened.

At one point during his contemplation, he picked up a gun and shot himself in the head.

> From that point, I had a visit from a lady; don't know
> who it was to this day. She was not from real life. She
> had told me I am not supposed to be there, that what
> I had done is very wrong, and that she was going to make
> it right again . . . Then I spent the next two weeks in a
> nightmare kind of state, living with awful things. Unlike
> the first time I died, she told me if I ever take my life
> again, this is what I would have to live with for eternity.
> (Anonymous, 2004, March 30, 9:55 PM)

It is important to add that although this man's distressing experience seemed to be associated with his suicide attempt, research has shown that in general, people who attempt suicide are just as likely to report blissful NDEs as those who die of natural or accidental causes. And whereas research indicates that suicide NDErs are subsequently less likely than even the general public to attempt suicide again, they do so not out of fear but because, in their NDEs, they learned that their life—and every life—has meaning and purpose; that if they seek to escape life's difficulties through suicide, they will simply return in another life and resume where they left off; and that difficulties are not to be escaped from through suicide but, rather, worked through as opportunities for spiritual development. Some of these principles are illustrated in the next case.

Unhappy Marriage and Alcohol
Another man (*Suicide NDE*, n.d.), in the throes of alcoholism and following an unhappy marriage, attempted suicide. He sped rapidly through a tunnel, at the end of which he saw a light. At the same time, when he looked back, he could see his body passed out on his kitchen floor. It made him wonder whether this was death.

"No!" came an answer from somewhere. I was shocked to see a being of incredible beauty, radiating great love, great compassion and warmth . . . I realized that my thoughts were being read by this incredible being of light. "No!" he repeated. "This is not what death is like. Come, I will show you." I remembered floating with him over to a pit of some sort that contained a very depressing scene of a landscape devoid of beauty, devoid of life, where people shuffled around with their heads down and their shoulders bent forward in a depressed, resigned manner. They kept their heads down and looked at their feet and wandered around aimlessly, bumping into each other occasionally but they kept on going. It was a horrifying thought that I was going to be cast down with these confused lost souls, but the voice seemed to understand my terror and relieved it with the following words: "This is a Hell of your own creation. You would have to go back to earth eventually and experience a new life all over again faced with the same difficulties that you faced in this lifetime. You will stay with these lost and confused souls until then. Suicide is not an escape."

He was given a panoramic view of his life. He saw various outcomes. In the first, his children would suffer due to his death. The second outcome was that he survived but continued drinking, which would also impact his children negatively, and they, too, would become alcoholics. The third outcome was that he stopped drinking and began to act like a responsible father. This would not be easy, but his children would have happy, busy, productive lives. He was allowed to go back to his life.

He wrote that he chose the difficult path, which would not only end in a divorce but also put a stop to his drinking habits. His children have since become happy, busy, and productive individuals.

A WAY OUT

Addicted to Crime and Violence

The quotes from the following NDE are from a person (Anonymous, 2012, July 10) who wrote that, from the age of eight, he was addicted to substances. From the age of 16, he needed more money to meet his need for alcohol and drugs. Crime and violence followed, including more than 30 bank robberies and several stints in prison. He wrote that although he was not "a poster child for a trip to heaven" . . . "God forgave me." One day, following excessive alcohol consumption, he suffered internal bleeding of the liver and had his NDE.

> While my body was out, my spirit was sent to hell. It was worse than I would have ever imagined. Besides the extreme uncomfortable feeling, I could not take a moment without being bumped into and grunted at. There were dark clay boxes of heat the size of an old 27-inch TV, and they were being moved around. It was crowded and you could not make out the faces. I could not tell if they were white, African American, or Asian. They were just there. At this point I started screaming to God to please forgive me. The grunting got louder, and I asked the Lord to please let me repent if I was to stay here. At that moment a light shined through, and I gravitated toward it.

He was in hospital at the time of his distressing NDE, and within 24 hours of his experience, he underwent surgery during which he had another medical crisis and a second NDE:

131

But this time when I died, there was a glorious light shining, not bright but almost enveloping my soul. I was slowly moving upward and never felt more at peace in my life. I just kept thanking God and praising him as I was being elevated. This was no dream.

Churchly Sounding Phrases

Another brave person who wrote about his distressing NDE is Howard Storm (2005). In his extraordinary book on this subject, *My Descent Into Death*, he described his distressing NDE, which he called his fall into hell.

In a hospital in Paris, he almost died from a gastric perforation. After he left his body, he became very confused. He tried to communicate with his wife, who was sitting beside his hospital bed, but, of course, she didn't hear him. He was bewildered. Seemingly friendly voices lured him away from his bed. Because the experience was so very real, and because he was a confirmed atheist, he didn't think of the possibility of being in his afterlife; rather, he thought he was hallucinating because of his illness. After a while, the voices gradually became antagonistic and authoritarian. A sense of dread grew in him. Then, suddenly, he realized he was in complete darkness, and insults started. Next, he was pushed around in the dark. The situation became ever more aggravating. He started to fight back. They started to bite and tear him and seemed to have great fun.

They were playing with me just like a cat plays with a mouse. (p. 17)

He described the creatures as "once human." He said they could be thought of as

the worst imaginable persons stripped of every impulse of compassion. Some of them seemed to be able to tell others what to do, but I had no sense of there being any organization to the mayhem. They didn't appear to be controlled or directed by anyone. Simply, they were a mob of beings totally driven by unbridled cruelty. (p. 17)

He explained in his book that because he did not want to recall and relive all of the profound torment he experienced, the description of his ordeal is not complete.

In fact, much that occurred was simply too gruesome and disturbing to recall. I've spent years trying to suppress a lot of it. After the experience, whenever I did remember those details, I would become traumatized. (p. 18)

He also said that the experience was far worse than any nightmare, because it seemed more real than being awake. It was hyperreal.

While his tormentors were swarming around him, he heard a voice—which sounded like his own—saying that he should pray to God. At first, he thought it was a stupid idea, but after he heard the voice a few more times, he tried. He murmured some churchly sounding phrases, and even the line with reference to God from the U.S. Pledge of Allegiance. This made the demons angry, but they retreated, nevertheless.

Because he recited the phrases without real sincerity, the retreat of the gruesome creatures was all he could do. Although he felt they remained near, he was alone. After he thought for a while about his miserable situation and about his egoistic life, which he started to regret, he made a genuine effort to pray. He prayed to Jesus, because that was the first person who came into his mind. After all, before becoming a committed atheist, he had been brought up Christian. Then, far off in the darkness, he saw a pinpoint of light rapidly coming closer. When it was near, he saw that it was the one he had been calling for, Jesus, who finally brought him out of his miserable position into the Light.

A Second Layer of Light Beings

This account is from one of the oldest documented and best known NDEs, described in the book *Return From Tomorrow*. In 1943, during World War II, George G. Ritchie (2004) was a soldier. He began his training in Texas, where he was subsequently exposed to dust storms, heavy rain, and a temperature of 10° F (–12° C). His throat started to feel sore, and soon he had developed a fever with a temperature up to 102° F (39° C). Within a few more days it ran up to 106.5° F (41° C). Later his fever was diagnosed as double lobar pneumonia.

His NDE started when he thought he was waking up. There was nobody around him. He went into the corridor. He saw a sergeant approaching and tried to draw his attention. The sergeant just kept on walking as if he didn't see Ritchie, and Ritchie had to jump out of his way.

Then it became even stranger. Within days, Ritchie was supposed to show up for his study at the Medical College of Virginia, to become a doctor registered on the Army Specialized Training Program. He desperately wanted to go there, so he rushed outside. Without realizing, he found himself "flying" eastward about 500 feet in the air. He was utterly surprised by his very high speed and that he could reach this velocity of his own accord without being in an airplane.

He found his way back to his body but was confused about the separation between his thinking self and his physical part. Then he started to see the Light, whose brightness increased. It seemed to come from nowhere, but it shone everywhere at once. It was like a million lamps, and then he saw it was not a light but a man. The awesome certainty came over him when he heard: "You are in the presence of the Son of God." He immediately knew that this man loved him unconditionally. He had a very detailed life review (see Chapter 6).

Jesus took him on a tour into hell-like situations and environments. At first, Ritchie was shown people who had already died but who seemed not to accept the fact. It felt a bit like the sergeant who hadn't seen Ritchie in the corridor, except that these people seemed to be stuck in some kind of self-created situation. One was still craving for cigarettes, others craved alcohol, while another still wanted to exert influence on the people he had left behind after he had died. Ritchie suddenly remembered a line from the Bible: "Lay not up for yourselves treasures on earth! For where your treasure is, there will your heart be also!"

Secondly, Ritchie saw people that he understood had committed suicide. They seemed to be chained to all the consequences of their act. Some begged to be forgiven, but, of course, their loved ones couldn't hear or see them because they were dead.

Lastly, he was taken to a place where there were no living people. There he saw a gruesome scene. The plain was crowded, even jammed, with hordes of ghostly discarnate beings. He carefully looked to see if there were any living people among the hordes, but he didn't see any:

> All of these thousands of people were apparently no more substantial than I myself. And they were the most frustrated, the angriest, the most miserable beings I had ever laid eyes on . . . everywhere people were locked in what looked like fights to the death, writhing, punching, gouging . . . And then I noticed that no one was apparently being injured . . . And the thoughts most frequently communicated had to do with the superior knowledge, or abilities, or background of the thinker. (pp. 63–64)

He then understood that he was no better than these ghosts, because he had similar thoughts of superiority:

> This was me, my very tone of voice—the righteous one, the award-winner, the churchgoer. (p. 65)

Ritchie also noticed that here there was no condemnation from the one at his side. He felt that it was not His desire, either, to see any of the other unfortunates in their unhappy state. He wondered how it was possible that the deceased could not see the incredible brilliance of Jesus's Light. But then he remembered that when he desperately wanted to go to the Medical College of Virginia, he couldn't see Jesus either. He was too preoccupied with his own desire. He then asked himself, "Perhaps it was not Jesus who had abandoned them, but they who had fled from the Light that showed up [in] their darkness."

Then he realized that there was a second layer over the horrifying plane he saw. Beings made of light were hovering above all that fighting:

> All I clearly saw was that not one of these bickering beings on the plain had been abandoned. (p. 66)

The beings of light had been there all the time, just as they had been there with the deceased he had previously seen. He said that he had

> been seeing them all along, without ever consciously registering the fact, as though Jesus could show me at any moment only so much as I was ready to see. (p. 67)

Ritchie concluded that it is *we* who, through physical appetite, earthly concern, and self-absorption, create the separation that blinds us so that we cannot see the Light.

I Don't Want to Be There

One summer evening as a child, Marijke Redant (n.d.) went cycling. She was making great speed, but suddenly the brakes locked, and she flipped over. After her head hit the asphalt, her light went out. Suddenly she found herself in a dark void, which was quite frightening. She determined that she was not alone there.

> There was an entity there that was so morbid, so murderous, so terrifying that it crossed my mind that I don't want to be here. And the moment you think in that other dimension "I don't want to be there," you move on. You're leaving that space where you are.

Then it turned light again, and the remainder of her experience was blissful.

OTHER VIEWS OF HELL

Creatures in a Waiting Room

> When we passed that dark area, it was as if the being of light that accompanied me, aroused these creatures. It seemed as if they had been asleep. It could also be that they were in a kind of waiting room. When they noticed us, they raced towards me. At first it frightened me, but the being of light that was holding my hand, told me not to be afraid and to look. Indeed, they came close, very close, but they couldn't touch me. I knew that if they wanted, they could come with us and be in the light. But they didn't want to. Or maybe they were not yet ready for it. (Coppes, 2011, p. 120)

Multidimensional Heaven

I realized that "heaven" was not one homogenous mass of existence but a multi-dimensional plane of layered existences . . . (Suleman, 2004, p. 27)

I was nevertheless acutely conscious of the fact that "hell" was definitely a state of mind that existed for many. It existed mostly for those individuals who did not believe in a higher power than themselves, nor felt themselves personally accountable to anyone for their actions. (p. 28)

As I looked below me to the left, I could see several groups of self-absorbed individuals completely wrapped up in their fourth dimensional world of created thought forms. They seemed totally oblivious of my existence or the existence of a higher realm of reality other than their own. They were caught up in their own little world and heaven of their own making, stuck in their rigid beliefs of "reality" and quite unaware of the greater reality existing outside their own little spheres of existence. From my perspective they were merely spinning their wheels, as they chased incessantly after their illusions of fame, power, grandeur and glory, and the utopian ideals of their self-made "paradise." (p. 33)

Free to Choose

Although Deirdre DeWitt Maltby (2012) had a blissful NDE, in her book she wrote something interesting about the difference between light and darkness:

Perhaps there is divine judgement in some way, but I was not shown that. I was only made aware that each person is free to choose where he or she wishes his or her internal self to be. We are still loved no matter what, but the existence we will find ourselves in will mirror the level of light and understanding we choose to play out in our earthly lives. We may choose to exist somewhere between brilliant light of complete understanding to the complete darkness of ignorance with all the unaccountable layers in between. (pp. 51–52)

— THERE IS NO PURGATORY AND NO HELL —

The final quotes in this chapter I find very interesting. They are from Chris Carson, and they are quite relevant with respect to distressing NDEs. The quotes are taken from the book *When Ego Dies* (Corcoran, 1996, pp. 33–38). The story can also be found in Liz Dale's (2008, p. 11) book about 21 gay people's NDEs.

As a 26-year-old, Chris Carson was heavily involved in alcohol. One night he was driving a car and thought about his life, his poor relationship with his father, being gay, and being worth more dead than alive. He convinced himself how utterly useless his life was. Then it occurred to him that his life insurance policy was worth more than his life. Sobbing in the driver's seat, he saw a concrete highway barrier and decided to turn the wheel and drive into it as fast as possible.

After the collision it was dark for a while, but then he ended up in a dark tunnel.

> Then I was surrounded by light, so intense I could feel it. I could not look, it just permeated me. I felt this enormous love and well-being—peace—if you will. I had some sense of omniscience, or knowing everything. I felt that everything was right—as it should be. There was a purpose to everything . . . There was absolute understanding, absolute love, absolute peace. (Corcoran, 1996, p. 35)

Although he was not Catholic, he received an explanation of hell and purgatory. The two accounts of Carson's experience in the two books mentioned above contain a contradiction: in one case a reference to "heaven," in the other to "purgatory." So, I asked him which was correct, and he clearly said, "no purgatory and no hell." Therefore, the correct quote is:

> I heard that really there is no purgatory and no hell. People who leave too soon [meaning suicide, like his own] or hurt others may (must?) watch what effect their action have on others . . . Watching the results can be painful, I understood, but I did not understand it to be mandatory. I just understood it—no purgatory or hell. The good ones get to watch, too. (Corcoran, 1996, p. 35)

He understood that there were plans for his life, which he had impacted through his suicide. He had to go back because there was much for him to do. He said that he departed from that other world while hearing the words, "Show them the way." (Corcoran, 1996, p. 36)

In the middle of surgery on his jaw, he woke up and startled the medics. He said about his own condition:

> My face looked like a Frankenstein, split between the lip and chin all the way to both ears, cuts and wounds all over. But I was at peace. (Corcoran, 1996, p. 36)

Similar messages can be found in other NDEs, for example:

> I was shown there is no hell. We all go home. (Anonymous, 2012, July 21)

CONCENTRATE ON LOVE, ON THE LIGHT

At the end of this chapter with some impressions of distressing NDEs, three conclusions seem warranted. The first is to move away from the explanation that distressing NDEs relate to guilt and punishment, because there is growing evidence that this explanation is incorrect.

The second is that we seem to have some control over our afterlife experience. During their NDEs, some people had the ability to go where they wanted to go or to shape the environment they were in. An example is George Ritchie (see above) who desperately wanted to go to Virginia where he had an appointment and found himself flying there in a great hurry but without an airplane. Other examples can be found in Chapter 3, in which Nancy Rynes and Ellyn Dye seemed to be able to exercise some influence over their surroundings.

In particular, in some of the distressing NDEs, the situation changed for the better after the experiencer asked for God, prayed, or sang a religious Christmas carol. The implication is that if one finds oneself in a distressing after-death situation, one might be able to move beyond that scenario by concentrating on love, on the God of one's religion, and/or on the Light.

The third conclusion is to always bear in mind the most important implication of NDEs, as discussed in Chapter 4: the notion of unconditional love for all and everything. Unconditional means without condition: no matter what we have done in our lives and no matter the situation we have created. Unconditional love is there for everyone—without exception! If there were exceptions, the love would not be unconditional.

Readers who believe that NDEs are actually a first step into the afterlife can trust that eventually everything will turn out right for everyone. And to top that off, the next chapter provides support for the conclusion that we are all ONE and are ONE with the Light. If we are ONE, then how could one part of that Oneness be left in distress?

CHAPTER 9

Interconnection With All and Everyone: We Are ONE

By far the most important feature of NDEs is the huge and unconditional love that experiencers have felt. In Chapter 4 I also stated that the other very important feature is the deep interconnectedness between everything and everyone that experiencers have reported. A summary of several special NDE aspects seems to point to this phenomenon of interconnectedness.

Many NDErs have reported that in their NDEs, all knowledge was freely available, including instantaneous answers to whatever questions they asked. They described communication with the Light or light beings as telepathic, that is, direct and instantaneously mind-to-mind. During their NDEs, time was not an obstacle, and it seemed that all time occurred at the same time. They encountered no physical barriers, being able to move around without difficulty, and they could observe anything instantaneously from all angles and in a variety of ways. Many experiencers reported feeling themselves as part of a huge energy and consciousness. And in my opinion the most striking aspect of NDEs is that during their life reviews, they felt what someone else felt as that very person.

All these aspects seem to imply that everything is deeply integrated. They imply that when we arrive on the other side of life, all knowledge is ours, all time is ours, and all locations are ours. We can completely identify with people we have met in life and experience their feelings as being them. We can even have this intense and direct contact with people who lived long before our time (see the Michelangelo example cited later in this chapter). And our bond with the Light and the beings of light is so strong and direct that when we communicate with them it seems as if they are in our minds and are directly connected.

Shouldn't we therefore conclude that we are at least very closely and very lovingly connected to all and everything? Indeed, many NDErs talk about a deep connection between all and sundry. And many NDErs go beyond that. They have concluded that we are at one with each other and with everything else. This unity and communion includes not only humans, animals, trees, planets, stars, and whole galaxies but also the world of Light and the Light itself. Everything is ONE.

See below the quotes that point in this direction. First are quotes indicating that we are part of a unified energy, that we are strongly interconnected and connected to our source or the Light. Therefore, it would be good for us if we aligned ourselves with the Light. Next are quotes conveying not only that we are interconnected with each other but that we actually *are* each other. Then there are quotes expressing that we are all part of a larger whole. And finally, there are quotes that take us one step further by asserting that each of us is, in part, God.

I realize this latter point may be too big of a step for some readers, but I must remain true to experiencers' quotes. Omitting these statements and their implications for all of us would render my impressionist painting of NDEs incomplete and unfinished.

———— EVERYTHING IS CONNECTED ————

Like the Law of Conservation of Energy

Everything I do has influence on everything. Nothing is lost. It is a kind of law of conservation of energy. That is why we shouldn't do to others what we don't want for ourselves. Moreover, what we send, we'll attract. We should also be mindful of our thoughts, because we create with our thoughts. (Coppes, 2011, p. 165)

Ripple Effect

A person who attempted suicide described the effect of her attempt as follows:

> My mind became acutely aware of the pain and suffering born out of my choice of self-destruction. [I understood] how my actions were like stones tossed into a pond. They rippled out, crossing over the entire surface of the earth, forever affecting and changing the face of it. (Futrell, 2003, p. 9)

——————— INTERCONNECTED ———————

> I felt a great sense of interconnectedness and oneness with everything in the universe. I no longer feared death because it was so patently obvious that death was illusory. (Anonymous, 2020, April 19)

Part of the Same Source

After a woman's surgery, she had an infection and had to go back to the hospital. When she arrived, everything went wrong. While her body was shutting itself down, she felt herself leaving it.

> I looked down at my non-physical arms and body. I saw an outline of form filled with golden white Light that radiated past the faint lines. As if I was a star shining brightly in the Heavens. The Light was fluid, iridescent and connected with ease to the Angels near or beside

145

me. I connected with the stars and the vastness of the Universe. I was a part of everything in existence all at the same time . . . I saw people as connected; all part of the same Source, but living different experiences. I understood how much of our experience is about choice; even when we decide to die. Every experience has purpose and helps us on our path to fulfill what we came here to do. There is no right or wrong, good or bad. It is only our perceptions that make it one way or the other. There is no one true religion or path to heaven. Whatever speaks to our hearts individually is the right path for us. All roads lead back to Source. (Anonymous, 2013, April 17)

You Always Remain Connected to the Whole

You are a piece of everything. A piece of the whole. You always remain connected to it. That piece goes back to that whole when you die . . . But what happens when I go through that door, I sometimes think about it. Because will I go through that door as myself, or will it only be my essence, I don't know. (Coppes, 2020, p. 145)

We Are Connected—We Are All One

During his NDE, Rene Jorgensen (2007) clearly felt that we are all interconnected and that we, in fact, are One (see chapter on life reviews):

The essence and purpose of life was love, but I had gone against love and therefore my own true nature. It was as if I had been doing all this to myself—by hurting others I had hurt myself. We are connected—we are all one. (p. 7)

146

Align Yourselves With the Light

In her book, Lee Thornton (2014) wrote that the experience led her to the belief that:

> The Light of divinity exists within all of us, that all discord arises from a sense of separation from the Light, and that as we align our minds and hearts with it [the Light], we can experience its qualities in the forms of peace, love, joy, compassion, and well-being. (p. 181)

I AM YOU, YOU ARE ME

I Am the Other and the Other Is Me

During the administration of anesthesia before her operation, Tetty Pols-Visser (Pols-Visser & Oosterhof, 2010) felt dizzy. Everything started to turn, and she was sucked into a deep darkness. And then she found herself standing in a radiant light.

> I feel the Light flowing through me, and then I am overwhelmed with a feeling that is beyond anything else. It's Love. I feel the Love that emanates from it, and an infinite peace and tranquility descends in me. I feel completely perfect, completely one with the Light and the Love, and I know that it is God. I am in God and God is in me. We are One. Perfect unity. I am no longer alone. I don't long for anything else anymore. So, this is it. This is where I am supposed to be. Home. I'm finally home. (pp. 74–75)

Afterwards, when she told her husband what had happened, she said:

> I remember. I am the Light. I am the Love. I am the Life. (p. 80)

Later in her book she concluded:

> Just like I am no longer a total stranger to myself, people
> are no longer strangers to me. I am the other and the
> other is me. I recognize myself in the other and know
> that we are One, that each of us in our own appear-
> ance, in our own unique way, expresses an aspect of the
> One. I see everyone in their true form. We are children
> of God. God has put all of Himself in us. We carry the
> divine within us. That is our core, our true being. Love.
> (pp. 83–84)

I Became That Other

Kimberly Clark Sharp (2003) was lying on the pavement with
no breath and no pulse. People from the fire department were
trying to resuscitate her. At one point, she saw a man leaning
over her to give her mouth-to-mouth resuscitation. Through
his touch, she was able to enter her body again. But it also
made her observe and experience what was happening to
her and that total stranger. For a moment she was this other
person.

> I realized I knew everything about him emotionally. I
> could feel his nervousness and even his discomfort about
> performing this intimate, humane service in front of a
> gawking crowd. But it was his compassion, his love for
> me, a total stranger, that guided me . . . back into my
> body. (p. 27)

I Became Michelangelo

In her book, Liz Dale (2008) wrote about a man who had
an NDE in which he met a friend who had died just a few
days before (also see Chapter 3, *Out of This World*). That
friend, Richard, taught the NDEr how to experience and

apply the fluid, non-linear qualities of time to that extraordinary other world in which they found themselves. Richard demonstrated this ability by making the NDEr go back to the time of Michelangelo:

> Somehow, he knew of my great passion for the artist Michelangelo. Suddenly, to my amazement, I was transported to the time and place where Michelangelo was painting the Sistine Chapel. For a fleeting moment I actually *became* Michelangelo. The experience was staggering beyond words. (pp. 100–101)

Another NDEr in Liz Dale's book said:

> I knew in my spirit that every person was connected to everyone else, that we were and I was a part of the living trees, plants, flowers, and oceans. I knew that everything was and is united in this universe. (p. 119)

I Merged With Jesus

Yvonne Sneeden's (n.d.) NDE occurred when her body was shutting down due to extreme emotional distress, the medication she was using, and her desire to just stop living. She was transported to a place she called heaven where she met Jesus who wrapped her in his love. As they walked through a magnificent landscape, they had a conversation. When she understood that she had to go back to physical life, she said that she was too tired and that she couldn't cope with so many mean, selfish, disloyal people on Earth.

He told her that he loved all of humanity and that he wanted to show her how much.

> He took my "heart" or my being, my identity, the energy that is me, and he merged with it, blended it with his

149

heart, and for a moment we were One. I exploded into the Light itself. I could feel all his feelings of love, it was mind blowing—Waves of love, of energy, millions of love related emotions, light, power, love. I was in the presence of the All and merged to such an indivisible consciousness that I became him. I was Jesus, the same way I was Yvonne, feeling every atom of this powerful boundless explosion of love, for lack of better words. It stopped suddenly and without a word, only knowing, I understood that my time with him in Heaven was coming to an end and it was time for me to return to Earth.

She said that heaven's love has kept her going with a complete renewed joy for her earthly life.

EVERYTHING IS ONE

Many Being One and One Being Many

The whole was the collective knowledge of all. I understood there was no individual, just one, yet each experience was individual making up the whole. This concept of ONE is so foreign to any description I can give, there seems to be no way of describing it . . . Many being one and one being many, both existing simultaneously in the same time and space. The collective experiences are omniscient knowledge. Everything that has been spoken, heard, and experienced. These colored drops contained each experience down to the memory of every cell division, every thought. All experiences were known at once by the collective consciousness that was the stream. Any experience could be known as if it were a first-person experience happening at the time it happened originally . . . I was shown a long line of experiences in other realms of realities and on other worlds.

It was some time later I realized it was my past "lives" review of all existences of which I had been part . . . I was made to know there were an infinite number of realms of existence and all were part of the One, the Source. (Anonymous, 2006, June 19)

One With All

Rachel Finch (2019) wrote her NDE in verse because she couldn't express her NDE in any other way. She felt she was at one with everything.

> In this space, I know each star by name,
> I house every memory ever made and
> I am high, looking
> below me,
> besides me and
> all I see is
> everything. (p. 46)

I Became Everything and Everyone

In my opinion the most special aspect of Anita Moorjani's (2012) beautiful book is that she speaks so clearly about the unity of everyone and everything. For her, that sense of unity began right after she left her body, which I described in the first chapter (*Out of the Body*), but because she put it so clearly into words, I repeat it here:

> As my emotions were being drawn away from my surroundings, I started to notice how I was continuing to expand to fill every space, until there was no separation between me and everything else. I encompassed—no, *became*—everything and everyone. (p. 64)

As she progressed further into her NDE, she found herself on the airplane her brother was taking (see Chapter 3, *Out of This World*), and she saw how badly he wanted to get to her hospital in time to see her before she died. But as she progressed even further into her NDE, that sense of unity grew, and her attachments decreased.

> As I continued to plunge deeper into the other realm, expanding outward, becoming everyone and everything, I felt all my emotional attachments to my loved ones and my surroundings slowly fall away. (p. 65)

She wrote that she felt that we are all connected. She called it the "interwoven unification" that encompasses everything, every human being, every animal, every plant, even seas and mountains—basically, the entire universe. Everything is One. She said:

> I realized that the entire universe is alive and infused with consciousness, encompassing all of life and nature. (p. 70)

She also met her father, who had passed away years before. They had an in-depth conversation, and she wrote that she not only understood him, but she *became* him. There was no difference or separateness between her and her father (p. 73).

After her NDE, she could no longer see duality in the world in which she and we all grew up. She expressed that there is no "me" and "you." There is no "perpetrator" or "victim." We are all of them at once. We are One (p. 109).

There Is No Friend and Enemy
During World War II, from age 3 to 6, Tienke Klein (2006) was interned with 3,000 Dutch women and children in a

Japanese concentration camp on Java, in the then-colony of the Dutch East Indies. The housing was a dilapidated barracks for up to 450 soldiers. The old pump did not provide enough water, and the toilets consisted of a small platform with a hole in it perched above a dry "kali" (a stream). Many women and children died of tropical diseases and starvation. At one point cholera broke out. Consequently, as a 4-year-old, Tienke suffered a cardiac arrest. Instantly she was in a dark, peaceful space where there was only Love. Her mother was a nurse and resuscitated her with salt water and cardiol injections.

Then Tienke returned to the hell of the camp. Two days later, still totally weak, she had to stand for hours at the daily roll call in the blazing tropical sun. She was at risk of fainting and realized the danger of being severely punished by the "Japs," as she repeatedly called the Japanese soldiers, for disrupting the roll call. She wrote:

> The moment my ears start ringing and the ground fell out from under my feet, I hear a voice. It is inside me, but I hear it loud and clear: "There is no friend and foe, that's a silly adult game, it is not the Truth."
>
> That's how it was there! And so, it is here now. An enormous strength and calm come over me. The danger has passed.
>
> I've changed forever. The camp no longer defines my horizon. Although as a child I no longer have any memory of the life outside the camp. A Space has come into me, which no one can take from me anymore.
>
> I have come Home, where there was no home anymore. This has become the hub of my life. This unconditional Love, which rises far above hatred and war. (p. 19)

Being at One With the ALL

Juliet Nightingale (Anonymous, 2002, February 5, 1:18 PM) described this aspect of her NDE:

> Now I was acutely aware of the divine Presence, the Creator and spirit guides all round me. There was a profound realization of never being alone and always being in communion with Spirit and other beings in this awesome and magnificent realm. The most profound aspect of the NDE, for me, was that of being completely enveloped in divine Love and also being totally free of fear! There was no question that Love was everywhere, that I was completely protected and safe, and that everything would work out just as it should. There was never a feeling of being "isolated" or alone. This was a special opportunity to experience being at one with the ALL—never separate, and never at a loss. I knew—with total certainty—that everything was evolving exactly the way it should, and that the ultimate destiny for every living being is to return to the Source, the Light . . . Pure Love.

We Are the Entire One

Yazmine Star (*Yazmine S NDE*, n.d.). related her NDE in this way:

> I was flying through Goldenness: pure, serene, and delightful Goldenness. Oh, wow! I was held by this serenity for the longest time, I couldn't do anything except be with It and It with me. It was inside me. It was me. It was in and with everyone and everything. It had always been in and with everything. It was and is Truth, Love, Compassion, Joy, and All. This Goldenness held all information. It was the One Mind. It contained the

creation of all of everything ever created. I felt, I experienced everything that has ever been and ever shall be. All is simultaneously occurring. There is no past or future. It all just IS. . . .

I saw we are not separate; we are the entire One. I saw that we must have all the courage possible to achieve this fabulous unity. It is highly possible. . . .

I felt and experienced all of creation as an Omni-experience, there was no time involved at any level. I saw it is so simple it cannot be expressed.

All Is Everything, Everything Is One

I remembered that I had a daughter, and before I could plead my case for returning, I was told by thought that I would not be allowed to stay. I got excited to return, and thought how much I wanted to remember the knowledge [she had gained during her NDE] so I could explain it to others, to ease fears of death, and inspire goodness. I thought that maybe I could trick them. I would think of some words that perfectly described the knowledge in its simplest form, and then remember the words. Then I'd associate the words and remember the knowledge. I came up with perfect words, All is Everything, Everything is One. I was so happy with my choice of words. I knew that I would remember. (Anonymous, 2009, April 18)

Place of Oneness

In her book, Azmina Suleman (2004) wrote she saw different dimensions. She described the fourth dimension as the dimension immediately adjacent to our physical three-dimensional world of matter. She said it is the dimension of our thoughts, primarily our notions of separateness. When we can see through the "illusions" of separateness, we can

"move forward and reach that ultimate place of 'Oneness.'"
(pp. 58–59)

Part of a Larger Life Force

A Muslim man (*Caan S NDE*, n.d.) fell from a ladder and landed head-first on a concrete surface. In his NDE:

> I got the impression that we are all part of a much bigger picture that God (Allah) has in store for us all. One of the opening verses in the Qur'an, first chapter, states that God (Allah) is Lord of all the worlds. . . .

He went on to say:

> I truly do believe that Allah (God) has given man many roads to get to him and none has a monopoly on Heaven . . . everything travels on one bandwidth back to Allah (God). Life exists in ways and places we have no knowledge of but to respect it all the same; because the sources are all the same. We, mankind, are part of a larger life force built on a big heap of love and knowledge all for one purpose to praise the Creator.

Riddle of Life

In his NDE, an Indian homeopathic physician (*India physician NDE*, n.d.) understood that if he wanted to, he could go back to his body. But he had to be quick. Apparently, if he waited too long, the way back would be blocked. Other NDErs have also described the risk of not being able to go back again. In this case, however, the man desperately wanted to know "an answer to the riddle of Life" before he returned to his body. He got the answer in a wonderful image:

> There was a beautiful vision of stars roaring past me. At the center of all that tumult was a glowing light. Each star appeared to be a minute center of consciousness. It was merging into and emerging from the central consciousness as desired by that cosmic WILL which shone like a very huge sun!

The image implies that we all come from the same source, that we all go back to it, and that together we form the central consciousness. In other words: We are one.

WE ARE PART OF GOD

An Interview With God

Brooke Jones (2021, 2023) had her NDE after an overdose of drugs and found herself talking to no less than God himself who welcomed her on His doorstep. (Although she referred to God as "Him" and "He," God assured her that He is genderless). At first, she asked if she could make a deal with Him, but God jokingly turned down that offer. Apparently, one cannot negotiate with God or make a deal. Therefore, because she was a journalist, she asked if she could at least have a talk. He granted that request, allowing her to interview Him and ask numerous questions.

His answers turned out to be with a great sense of humor. Later, she said that God met her at her level and presented Himself in a way that was not threatening but, rather, was warm and loving. Based on all of her Q&A, Jones (2021) wrote a very humorous book, *Why Are There Monkeys? (And Other Questions for God)*.

She didn't see God but only heard Him, and she heard Him in a manner that she couldn't really describe, but it was as if God's voice was within her. Therefore, the first question was about His appearance and what to call Him. The answer was that He is a spiritual being having no gender and that humans' name for Him does not define Him. Then she posed the question about the monkeys and evolution that resulted in the title for her book. Other questions were, for example, about God's accountability for the cruel acts committed by people, often in the name of religion. The answer was that people have their own responsibility, and there is free will. God said:

> Fate is one of man's most clever inventions. It is a tool by which he [a human] frees himself of responsibility for his actions. (p. 80)

Regarding religion, God said that it is a human-made concept:

> It is a collection of rites and rituals, dogmas and edicts, all invented by men to control other men. It has nothing whatsoever to do with Me. (p. 50)

He also assured that He answers all prayers no matter from what religion. Why? "Because there is only Me."

Jones asked where our energy goes after we die, and the answer was, "It merges with the energy of the universe, like a thread blending into a tapestry" (p. 67). Then she asked what the soul is. The answer was that it is a combination of that energy and Spiritual Essence, which is part of Him. "In fact, it's the cord (so to speak) that connects us to Him . . . In us is a part of Him, and He lives forever" (p. 67).

Eight earthly minutes resulted in lots of interesting questions and joyous answers. In the epilogue, she explained why the Q&A with God was real without any doubt and wasn't caused by the hallucinations of a dying mind. What that fantastic evidence is makes for a wonderful read that I highly recommend.

The Word "God" Is Too Small

After Brigitte Buyle (n.d.) had her life review in which everything she had done was accepted, she felt the love of all those light beings who had joined her in viewing her life review. She reported in an online video:

> I returned that love and I became that love. I became only love and there was no more difference, there was no distinction, it was all one, but all was love. And I must be honest, both people and animals and everything, everything was love. There is nothing without love. It's very strange. Ultimately what we see is materialized love, but we don't realize it. . . .
>
> Your identity does not disappear, but you dissolve. So, for people who are very attached to how they are and who they are and their status, this is actually threatening, I think, because you dissolve. . . .
>
> Our word God is too small. Even if you make it bigger, it is still too small. It's . . . everything! It's everyone, but also everything. So strange . . . It's you and me, and the cat [the video shows her cat trying to get her attention], it's everything!

We Are ONE With God

A Jewish man (*Shalom G NDE*, n.d.) had two NDEs. The second NDE was quite complete with a life review and a meeting with deceased relatives. He encountered a very special being and asked him whether he was Jesus. The being replied that he was called "by many names" and that the NDEr could call him "Big Brother." When the man decided to go back to Earth, he was asked to instruct others that:

> GOD cannot be put into a box or labeled. GOD is NOT only one religion, but ALL religions. We are not separate

people on this planet, but [we are] ALL His children, connected by the Spirit of GOD within. And, last but not least, in order to have Faith in GOD we must have faith in ourselves, for we are ONE with the BIG GUY!

I No Longer Exist as a Separate Entity

Barbara Rommer's (2000) book on distressing NDEs includes a wonderful story by a native American woman called Sadhana who was studying in India. For me, this story says it all.

Sadhana had her NDE after drinking some contaminated water. She shot up to the Light and went "beyond time" and eventually "beyond space." She went "beyond having any body whatsoever," after which she had "only awareness." She said:

> Dropping the body gives such a freedom of not being confined! . . . As you rise further, you come in such bliss, not joy, but I mean bliss. Then you go further, beyond even experiencing, and you find it is a freedom to have no emotions, no experiences. If you keep going to The Light, and I hate to use the word "I" again [because she considers the "I" to have been dissolved], but I went all the way to the Godhead. Boy, that's not even the right word, but anyway, I went to the place where I no longer exist as a separate entity. It's like a drop in the ocean. You are totally dissolved. There is no separate consciousness. There is a vastness, and you are dissolved in whatever words we use for the Godhead. (p. 137)

I Am the Light of God

I viewed my life and several events and realized that we are all one with the Universe, so when I hurt someone, I was really hurting myself and even more so, I was hurting every soul in the Universe. I realized I was pure white light . . . There is no right and wrong as God said: "Heaven is not a gated community; it is open for all to enter here." God's gift of truth and love (goodness over doubt) helped me to stop doubting myself; I came to know that I am the light of God. (Anonymous, 2013, April 30)

Like a Grain of Sand on the Beach
One of the 50 NDErs interviewed in Mally Cox-Chapman's (1995) book said:

Suddenly I was there. In a sort of grey area, with light above me. Then I realized where I was, I saw the Earth. I understood that I was with God as I imagined Him, all knowing and omnipotent—that's what I was. Yet at the same time I realized that I was part of the Light, of God in general, like a grain of sand from the beach. I was a grain that was a God, but God himself was the whole beach. (p. 80)

One With the Force of God
In her book, Deirdre DeWitt Maltby (2012) wrote of this aspect of her NDE:

I was at this point coming to realize my unlimited potential as a human . . . I had the ability to create unbounded beauty in thoughts, words, and in deeds. I saw the ultimate potential of all humans yet how restricted we are—basically by our own limited thinking and actions. I let go, and in the letting go it was as if my *Self*, as an ultimate human, emerged. I found I was then co-creator with God. I was not anywhere near the magnitude of God but was *one with* that force. (pp. 55–56)

161

God Is in Everything and Unites Us All

Carol Lynn Vengroff (2012) wrote how she felt completely united with all and everything. She felt together as one. She called this the "God realization" (pp. 29–30).

> I also understood how God was in everything and united us all! (p. 14)

> I was keenly aware that I wasn't just me anymore. I was part of a love-bond without boundaries, in a perfect relationship that transcended time and form. (p. 23)

The All That Is

In describing her NDE, Ellen Dye (2023) said:

> It was like being in the Heart of God, totally embraced in pure unconditional love and joy! . . . I knew suddenly that I was back inside God, where I truly belong, where all of us truly belong. I realized, or remembered, that God is not a person or personality, even though humans like to portray "Him" as that . . . The God I was experiencing is All That Is . . . God IS Everything including each one of us. God is the Creative Force of all the Universes, a giant ocean of LOVE, from which all matter is created. And I was a little drop of that ocean, that once had been separated and was finally back where I belonged.

All Together We Are God

An anonymous NDEr (2018, June 30) reported:

> I could see pinpoints of light (stars) in the distance, but I was in a safe, warm embrace, filled with complete knowledge, total joy/ecstasy, and I was at one with everything. I was consciousness itself, back to my home.

My soul and everyone's soul were one. We are God, all of us. All knowing, all seeing. I had gone from profound separateness to profound inclusiveness in an instant. I suddenly understood that old saying that life is but a dream. That deep space blackness was the real world; this human world is just a dreamlike state of being. Yes, we are all dreamers in the same dream.

One With the Light

Rachel Finch related the following description of her NDE:

It was as if I "merged" with the light. It absorbed me, I absorbed it, we became One, completely . . . I was communicating with the light as well as experiencing being within it and One with it. (Anonymous, 2019, June 10)

No Hierarchy

In his book, Andy Petro (2014) wrote extensively about how he felt being in the Light (see also Chapter 5). He was a "holographic piece of the Light." There was no hierarchy, no judgment, no separation. He wrote:

I am not greater than nor less than the Light. In some way incomprehensible on earth, I am the Light, too. No matter how often I remember my Light experience, I always remember hierarchy does not exist in the Light; only oneness exists. (Locations 406–410)

Andy also had a life review (see Chapter 6), and he said that it was a perfect example of what "Oneness" feels like in the Light because he could see and relive all thoughts and feelings of all those he interacted with. It enabled him to see himself through the eyes and feelings of others.

A young woman NDEr echoed Andy's sentiment:

There was a feeling of everyone being connected and one with God and each other. (Anonymous, 2021, January 28)

. . . as did Rachel Finch:

I was completely at One with all of existence. (Anonymous, 2019, June 10)

. . . and Carol Vengroff:

My very essence was totally, wholly and absolutely in peace. I had dissolved into the I AM! [In the Jewish Bible God, or rather JHWH, refers to itself as "I Am" or "I Am who I Am"]. (2012, p. 30)

Separateness Brings Suffering

During her NDE, which she had after an attempted suicide, Sandra Rogers (1995) understood that we are all very closely connected. Everything we do impacts the whole of existence. She thought it was very important that we understand this. She said that our sense of separateness causes us to hurt each other:

[The] sense of separateness, I was shown, brought suffering into the world. (p. 56)

Her view is interesting because she links the sense of separateness to sin:

Sins are actions, or inactions, that hurt you and others . . . I saw that the sense of separateness causes us to hurt one another because we don't realize that when we only look to our self-interest, without considering the effect on others, we are actually exercising self-destructive behavior without consciously realizing it. (p. 56)

To put it differently, when someone hurts others, they unknowingly hurt themself, and that is because there is no separation between each other. She also said that "our soul is a part of the body of God," and "just like the smallest atom of your physical body is part of you, you are part of God" (p. 24)

These testimonials point to the conclusion that to become happier and to improve ourselves, we need to be more aware that there is no separateness between ourselves and others and that we are all a part of the Light.

CHAPTER 10

Why Are We on Earth?

Why are we on Earth? It is an interesting question, and in this Chapter I have put together some extraordinary answers that NDErs have received. Sometimes they explicitly asked this question, but other times the answer came as an unsolicited bonus in their NDE.

Many NDErs have returned with the understanding that the purpose of human life is to become more loving and to acquire knowledge. But it was an "eye opener" for me that many NDErs have also said that we are already perfect and, therefore, don't have to learn anything. From the start, we all are pure love, pure peace, and pure perfection—because we originate from the Light. We are part of it. We already have it in us. However, that divine love, peace, and perfection must still be expressed here on Earth, and that expression proves to be very difficult. This is because of all the limitations that exist, such as nature—for example, talents, capabilities, or defects that we are born with; nurture—for example, being born into a poor environment or a dysfunctional family; and the daily limiting dimensions of time and space.

From their point of view, we don't have to learn anything here on Earth. The purpose of life is to *express* that pure love, peace, and perfection. In other words, the goal of life is not a contract to learn something but, rather, is the journey itself.

So, life is about having experiences. Having experiences is important, and they are at their best when we can show the perfect love or the divine love that we all already have within us.

During an IANDS conference, I talked about the purpose of life with a few NDErs. At one point, one of them put it this way: "God got bored. God has gone to the movies." They meant that human existence is a form of "going to the movies" for God: having a thrilling experience trying to express divine love in a seriously limited environment. This idea is also reflected in the easy recipe for life that an NDEr received (see below). The recipe is available to all of us. It was very simple and consisted of four short points: experience life, just be, receive love, and give love. Only the latter two points require some effort.

PRE-BIRTH AGREEMENT

Agreed to Go Back

Some NDErs say that in their experience they learned that before being born into this physical lifetime, they essentially chose this life in order to experience and learn certain things that would contribute to their spiritual development. Nancy Rynes described this process eloquently in an interview available online (Chene, n.d.). She explained how, early in her NDE:

> There was a figure that came up to me from kinda off to the side. She seemed to just come out of nowhere . . . she gave me a big welcoming embrace of just love. And told me that she was going to be my teacher—that she would help me learn what I needed to learn in order to continue my life on Earth and make it one that I would be proud to live.
>
> And I kinda fixated on that. I said, "Wait a minute; you're going to send me back there? I don't want to go back there." And she said, "Well, you've already agreed to go back." And I told her, "I don't remember that. I didn't agree to it now. I don't remember agreeing to going back

there." She said, "Well, you agreed to do that before you were born." But my human self, Nancy, the atheist that I had just been, had never heard of [pre-birth agreements] before. So, I challenged her on it. I said, "Well, I don't remember agreeing to anything before I was born."

So, kind of in the air in front of me—it's very weird how this happened—but in the air in front of me, she showed me the time before I was born when I was agreeing to some of the things that I wanted to do and experience while I was in this life of Nancy. . . .

The teacher then showed Nancy some circumstances specific to her physical life.

And as soon as I saw this, basically in the air in front of me, all the memories flooded back. And I remember being in the presence of all of my spiritual teachers. And I guess you would call it "the presence of the Divine" was also there, and I agreed to these things. It's not like a contract, like where if you break it, you're going to be sued or anything. But it's really kind of a guidepost as to how you want to live your life. And so, if you don't do things, it's okay; you just, at some point, have to do those things. You know, that's what you want to learn; at some point, you're going to need to learn it, whether it's in this lifetime or some other way. So, I saw all that, and realized, "Well, okay, I guess I *do* have to go back because I agreed to go back."

ENJOY THE GAME

Experience and Enjoy Life
During four days of critical illness in the hospital, Kimberlee Anderson left her body, met her angels, and received

from them answers to some of her most essential questions, including:

> Our purpose here is to discover unconditional love within ourselves and then offer it to others. We are all on [this] path. What differs between us is the road we take, the experience we choose, and how much we have learnt about love. No one road is better or more important than another. It is all a matter of what speaks to your heart and feels like home within. We are here to explore, experience and find joy in the process of living an earthly existence. Our evolution and ascension as a spiritual being happens organically at a time when we are ready to receive it. We are all constantly growing, evolving, and changing. But this is not anything we have to force or for which we need a certain skill set. We are all spiritual beings having the human experience.

After she came back into her body, she recovered miraculously. She turned her life around completely. She wanted to live life to the fullest. She no longer cared about minor things, such as traffic jams or that someone pushed ahead of her in a line. Her motto became:

> If I am not going to remember this five years from now, I am not going to give it any more thought today. (Anonymous, 2013, April 17)

Playground

When Christina was eight years old, she was kidnapped by two men, during which she survived a near-drowning. Her NDE made a lifelong impression on her. She said that she probably thinks of her experience once each hour, if not more often. She also said:

It was not until a few years ago that I accepted being here. I even tried to commit suicide three times as a young adult to return. I still prefer not to be here, but I know that I don't have a choice. I know that I have a purpose—as if I have an assignment. It's to help others . . . not be afraid of the unknown; and help them to see the light in themselves. There are four lessons I learned from my NDE: 1) love, 2) be loved, 3) just be, and 4) experience life. The earth is our playground! Have fun! (Anonymous, 2012, November 18)

When I discussed this subject with Christina, she told me that the four points were very clear lessons given to her and meant to be taken back as a message. They came from the only being she spoke with during her NDE whom she calls "my Father" and considers to be God. The four points were given as if they were a recipe for life here on Earth. The last bit—about Earth being our playground—were her own words to express her thoughts at the time, and she added that it's no fun being alone on the playground. The idea is that we should not only experience life but also try to enjoy it as much as we can.

Entertainment

One NDEr had left his seriously ill body and reported that:

With one angel in front and two on the side, we went up high in the clouds. Then, we started moving horizontally, going faster than an airplane, and they did not need wings to fly. I thought to myself, "shouldn't friction be causing me pain from wind pressure?" The angel in front spoke without using his mouth. He stated, "There's no friction here." I said mind to mind why isn't gravity making me fall? He replied, "There's no gravity here." I remembered learning that temperature in the clouds is extremely cold and I thought why am I not cold? "There's no cold here" was the response. I started to think about my job and university and the angel told me "There's no stress here!" I asked, "Why aren't we talking with our mouths?" He responded, "On earth, talking with your mouth makes your throat dry." Then, I said to him, "I'm glad you speak English, how many languages do you speak?" He said, "All of them." I told him I wanted to ask some other things. I asked him for the meaning of life. He told me, "For the entertainment of the spirit realm." (Anonymous, 2012, January 3)

ALREADY PERFECT

No Good or Bad

Following a car accident, this NDEr left her body and, during her NDE, learned:

We (here on Earth) have a role to play. We choose our lives even before we are born . . . whether we chose a good life or a bad one . . . it matters not, because there is NO good or bad . . . it's just your chosen role . . . and ALL lives lived are essential for our evolution and development. That's why we have memory. WE LEARN AND GROW because we have different lifestyles, beliefs, opinions, etc. Sorry to say this, BUT even the evil—death, destruction, disease—is essential! Think about it, if everything was ALWAYS good and going your way, if all relationships were good and everyone got what they wanted, over the years it would get pretty boring and stagnant. I know, it sounds wonderful, but it wouldn't let us grow much, would it? (Anonymous, 2016, September 23)

Express Our Divinity

Lee Thornton described her conclusion following her encounters with the Light both during and after her NDE:

> I came to see the Light as the compassionate teacher that lives within each of us as our highest self. It seems to want us to experience its joy and wisdom, and to help us expand; to move beyond the limits and obstacles that prevent us from realizing the happiness and freedom we are capable of experiencing. I came to believe that the divinity of this Light lies in and around every individual, and it is our life's purpose to find and express that divinity which exists—not somewhere far away in some distant world, but right here, within each of us. (Anonymous, 2013, June 17)

Steeped in Unconditional Love

A wife and mother was critically ill with infected lungs and sinus cavities and a high fever of 103° F. In the hospital she had her NDE. After she recovered, she said:

> Today I enjoy perfect health in my physical body, but I know that who I really am is already in a complete state of perfection steeped in unconditional love. (Anonymous, 2012, September 1)

Live Heaven on Earth

While dying from cancer, Anita Moorjani had an NDE, during which, she said:

> The amount of love I felt was overwhelming, and from this perspective I knew my powerful nature and saw the amazing possibilities we as humans are capable of achieving during a physical life. I found out that my purpose

now would be to live heaven on earth using this new understanding and also to share this knowledge with other people. (Anonymous, 2007, April 26)

Be Happy

Yazmine Star reported that during her NDE:

> [I was] ashamed that I had not realized how impera-tive it is for one to be incredibly happy in this life, no matter the circumstances. The pain, the fear: no mat-ter what! All our material conflicts of body and mind are quite unimportant in the state of ultimate freedom and blissful awareness to which we shall all return. I felt I had been unfaithful to The Great Presence, who is like a divinely loving Mother, and who I had let down. I was my own judge. Yet I was this love simultaneously. I saw how all of Humanity has walked with eyes cast low to the Earth, not opening wide to the beauty of the one lov-ing presence of Golden peace. This peace is one in which we truly live, yet do not see. . . .
>
> I saw how in being uplifted we could all ascend to the true joy together as a loving family of Beings beyond a human life in mundane-ness. I saw how there is a level of fear so ingrained in some, it's hard to look at, and yet they too can find a way through to peacefulness. I saw how things will change, yet only after massive suffering and yet I saw, too, that it is possible to end suffering. (*Yazmine S NDE*, n.d.)

Free Will?

Several NDErs have assured me that each person has a task—a purpose—on Earth. One even said that you wouldn't be here if you didn't have a task. However, many NDErs also say that free will is not required to perform that task: The universe is guiding us. Everyone has an internal compass, and not following it is a waste of time and energy. The compass helps us fulfill our tasks because we are destined to achieve our goal. We just have to be aligned and in tune with the Light, and all will go smoothly. During an interview with NDEr Anna Best, she became emotional when I repeatedly asked her about free will. She said:

> In that other dimension free will is not important. It is important here, because it is related to [humans], to the ego of [humans], but I want to go with the universal flow. I don't want my free will to be in discord with universe. I don't want it to be in the way of my fulfillment. (Coppes, 2011, p. 80)

However, she stressed explicitly that her attitude had nothing to do with a lack of will. She said that sitting in a chair, waiting for universe to get her going was not what she meant. What free will meant to her is not to put her ego first. In her NDE, she had to let go of her ego, and that was what had felt right. Here, on Earth, she tries to let go as well.

―――――――――― FOR GOD ――――――――――

God Uses Us to Experience Himself
Tetty Pols-Visser shared this conclusion following her NDE:

> [God] wants to experience himself and does that through us. Through us, God can look at himself and become aware of himself. So, we are all aspects of Him . . . I have felt and know that we are One and that we are all a part of that One. My frequently asked question: Where is God? has been answered. God is all and in all. But that feeling sometimes seems unreal, far away. The

way I feel now [being back on Earth], I can hardly recognize God in it. (Pols-Visser, T., & Oosterhof, M., 2010, pp. 118–119)

Just Experiences

When Ellyn Dye (2023) saw all things she had thought, felt, and done "in every life I've ever had on Earth and on every other planet," she also saw the horrible things that had been done to her and the horrible things that she had done to others.

> And yet these amazing Beings loved me deeply, not in spite of all of it, but BECAUSE of all that I had done, and all that had been done to me, and because of all of Who I AM. There was absolutely no judgment at all, because all those experiences were just that: experiences. They were part of my soul's growth, because a soul grows through experience. And as I had experiences, God and All That Is had experiences through me.
>
> That is all part of the Divine Plan: all these little drops of the Divine Ocean separate themselves from the rest of the Ocean and go off to have all kinds of experiences, every type of experience that is possible. And because we are all connected, as we have an experience, everyone else and the whole Divine Ocean has the experience, too.
>
> They helped me deeply understand that All is Well, and that everything is going according to the Divine Plan. And they told me that the humans on planet earth are fast approaching a great shift in consciousness, when all the veils will be lifted and we will take off our masks and remember Who We Are, like revelers at a costume party, who pull off their masks at midnight . . . and here it is, 11:59 p.m. on planet earth!

LOVE

Practice Love

In her book, *Awakenings From the Light*, and her submission to the NDERF website, Nancy Rynes wrote that we are on Earth to Love:

> These experiences have opened my heart to all peoples, all faiths, and all beliefs in a way that I would not have thought possible. I will share a small bit of the first thing she [the spirit who accompanied Nancy] taught me. We are primarily here to Love: to practice Love, to show Love, to experience Love. Hate is not the language of Spirit, nor is fear. Love is. It is a Love that has no conditions or strings attached. It is simply Love in all of its forms. (*Nancy R NDE*, n.d.)

In her book she wrote about the lessons she learned from her Guide who accompanied her on her walk on "the Other Side, also known as Heaven:"

> We are not on earth to simply learn, but to love. We are on Earth to love everyone and everything. We are meant to find and experience joy in feeling and expressing love to others. It is through the acts of love and compassion that we are brought closer to our spiritual center, and to God. . . .
>
> It turns out that love is one of the main reasons for being on Earth. As love forms the structure of Heaven, it exists as an undercurrent in our world, too . . . Spiritual love doesn't mean loving just those people in our families, or simply loving people we agree with, but loving *everyone* and *everything*. That's Big Love, and it's not always easy for us humans to live this way . . . God

isn't simply asking us to love other people, but *all of* creation. The mountains, the air, the rain, the trees, the animals, and the stars are all connected spiritually . . . Yes, it is our choice to *practice* love in some form or another every day . . . In choosing to love as expansively as we can, we will likely need to learn how to let go of past hurts and to see beyond the surface, straight to the heart of people or situations . . . My Guide insisted that we try our best to extend love to everyone and everything on Earth: to you, your spouse or partner, friends, your siblings, the unfriendly neighbor down the street, the politician you don't agree with, those people across the sea that your country invaded last year, the folks with the skin color a shade or two different from your own, those who worship in a slightly different way from you, fans of the opposing team, and even the animals. All are a part of God and God loves all of them. In extending love to everyone and everything, loving *all* of creation, we therefore love *all* of Spirit. Not just parts of Spirit as most of us do now. *All* of Spirit. (Rynes, 2015, pp. 49–52)

As with many NDErs, Rynes has learned a lot from her experience. Her book is full of wonderful and wise perspectives that she received during her excursion into the other side of life or that she derived afterwards from thinking about her experience. When closing her book, she summarized some of this wisdom. One of the things she said is that life should not only be seriousness. Her advice is to enjoy life, as well, and to:

Listen to the calling of your heart, for in it is the key to happiness and fulfillment. It is one of God's ways of speaking directly to you. (Rynes, 2015, p. 220)

The Same Journey

In Liz Dale's (2008) book, one gay person who had an NDE said:

> We are here on earth to celebrate life, to love and help one another, and to tap into and use all the gifts and talents our creator has endowed us with, i.e., pursuing our "mission" on earth within the divine plan. Unconditional love applied on a daily basis is how we help ourselves to evolve and touch other people's lives. Giving and receiving are fused together. We each have our own unique path, yet we all are on the same journey: "conforming to the Creator's likeness, day by day . . ." and finally "going home." (pp. 59–60)

To Learn, to Love

Kimberly Clark Sharp (2003) summarized the essential conclusions from her NDE:

> I was learning the answers to the eternal questions of life—questions so old we laugh them off as clichés. "Why are we here?" To learn. "What's the purpose of our life?" To love. (p. 26)

Be the Love That We Are

The greatest revelation Anita Moorjani (2012) received during her NDE was that we humans are love. Without exception, pure love is within every person. It may not always be expressed easily or well, but it is there. In Chapter 4 about Unconditional Love, her views are quoted, including what she considers to be the reason for our existence on Earth:

> If we're all One, all facets of the same Whole, which is unconditional love, then of course *who we are is love*!

[Our purpose is] to be our self, live our truth, and be the
love that we are. (p. 76)

Help Each Other

A male graduate student, whose NDE occurred in the context
of heart failure, reported:

> My life review was, well, lengthy, so I can't go into it
> here. Yet, it happened in less than a second and I saw
> EVERYTHING I ever did, said, wrote, thought . . .
> embarrassing. We [he and a spirit guide whom he called
> the "Man"] mentally chitchatted a bit, and then he said,
> "Is there anything that you'd like to know?" I said, "Yes,
> the age-old question, Why are we here on earth?" The
> "Man" responded, "You are only here on earth for one
> reason. You're only here to help each other," almost cer-
> tainly implying that we are here temporarily, to serve
> that function. I presume for some higher purpose to be
> known in the future (after death). (Anonymous, 2006,
> January 30)

Love Is Made Manifest

One woman hemorrhaged during childbirth and had two
NDEs. During them, she received information about the
meaning of life. It had to do with manifesting love:

> I learned it is truly marvelous to be in spirit form, to be in
> my light body, unlimited, all knowing, unencumbered.
> But it is only in our human bodies that we can hold a
> newborn baby to our breasts, walk on a beach at sunrise,
> make love, smell a rose, or taste a strawberry. It is here
> in our bodies that the lessons of love are made manifest.
> It is on this marvelous human adventure that we actu-
> ally increase the God Consciousness, as co-creators . . .

whenever we choose Love . . . knowing of course that there is Free Will . . . there is rejoicing in Heaven every time I take a deep breath, with consciousness, I am remembering and renewing my spirit, my connection to Spirit, and the privilege of being alive. (Anonymous, 2017, February 17)

—— RAISE THE ENERGY, THE VIBRATION ——

Raise the Vibration

Carol Lynn Vengroff (2012) wrote a short but wonderful book about her NDE. In it she encouraged us to continue living our lives, because one of the many messages from her NDE was that:

Each and every one of us is here for a reason. Each of us has a gift to share, a creative talent, a contribution to make, a chance to raise the vibration of each other and our planet . . . It is all perfect, every single part of our life . . . every single incident, seeming coincidence, event, encounter and decision. Every single moment is part of a perfect plan, part of our journey, and we get all our answers in the end. (p. 73)

Create a Better World

When Bill Gladstone briefly passed out after having had a flu shot, he had the opportunity to connect to beings of Light that escorted him on a trip. In my unpublished interview of him, he described what he learned:

I have always felt my existence on earth is to bring joy and awareness to myself and others. My intuition tells me we are here to help human beings become more aware, kinder and more loving towards themselves and others. The NDE increased this inner sense of knowing which I have had even as an infant. I have always been aware on a deeper level that life is eternal and that each and every one of us has a purpose. Even or perhaps especially those we discount or disagree with have a purpose. It makes no difference whether we focus on a powerless homeless person or the most wealthy and powerful people on the planet. We are all connected to a divine and intricate pattern of life and evolution that is never ending. Life is magical and there are no limitations on what human consciousness can create and support. As human beings we are gifted with the opportunity to learn on both the micro and macro levels. We are human and we will make mistakes but we are human and we can learn from our mistakes. Compassion. Kindness. Faith. Joy. Love. These are the attributes to develop and cherish and in so doing we contribute to creating a better world in the immediate present as well as in the future.

Each Moment Is an Opportunity

In my unpublished interview with Gayle Gladstone, she described how, when she nearly drowned on Kauai and had her NDE life review, she understood that each seemingly insignificant moment of earthly life matters. In each moment there is an opportunity to shine Light, the Light that is within everyone. We all have the power within us to make a difference and to increase love in the world.

> Life is not just about doing good and living well. It is also about being present and helping the energy raise in every given moment. Who I am does make a difference. Loving Kindness and clear communication, whether with a kind word, smile, loving eye contact or a silent helping hand, I have the power to calm storms of unrest just with my

> intended heart. I have the power to tap into another by being present with my thoughts, words, and deeds. I can harness goodness and share by being here and now.

When she realized this truth, she wanted to return to Earth to put her newly acquired insights into practice.

> I decided to return. I wanted to be that person. I wanted to try. I knew within that there are so many possibilities to embrace.

Here is how she tries to live now:

> We are Beings of Light. There is a responsibility to accept the One within us that can harness the power to help and heal in every given moment anything.
>
> I walk with every step. I commune with nature and nature responds in extraordinary ways. My relationship with life is a partnership. My abilities are much more enhanced. I know there is a Universe that supports me and my intentions. My goal every day is to honor, learn and listen to everything around me. I pay attention and accept that I am a piece of an endless sea of potential. There is this amazing Consciousness that is all knowing and ever evolving with a Highness indescribable and a Love unfathomable. I am grateful to this Awareness each and every day, and I strive to be worthy of my life.

Choice of Emotions

Silvia Bulten-Bolk was a singer and an artist with a radiant energy, but her body was not cooperating (Coppes, 2011, pp. 75–76). When she was 33, she had to undergo major abdominal surgery. After the operation, she was taken to the

ICU where she was kept in a coma. There she had her NDE. She entered a dark room where she felt the protective arms of her previously deceased father around her. That was a great comfort to her. She literally heard the message, "Your father is here for comfort and trust." About that situation she said:

> All the while I was aware that I was not looking with my eyes, not hearing with my ears, not talking with my mouth, not smelling with my nose. The body was irrelevant, I didn't need it there at all. I was in a space, or rather a state, deep in my mind. It smelled of flowers, it felt warm and safe there, yes, it felt like I had come home.

She was given the choice of staying or going back. Meanwhile, the darkness became brighter, and she could see a long line of people, including uncles, aunts, and souls both known and unknown. She realized that from the age of 11 she had been tired due to all the pain and sorrow because of the limitations of her body. Staying "up here" seemed very attractive, but she thought of her great love, Robert. Then she heard:

> You can choose because your journey, your film need not be completed yet.

She chose to stay with her great love. It now is 22 years later; she thus is 55. She said:

> My life is far from easy because my body is my greatest life lesson. Again and again, it brings me challenges in the form of illnesses and deficiencies [for example, the operation during which she had her NDE left her with a colostomy].

What this NDE gave me is an endless trust in the "think spirit" and the conviction that we are not this body but a "think spirit" attached to the primeval source we call God. It made me aware that instead of choosing fear (all our negative emotions) at any time we can choose thoughts of Love, which is God and which is us. It convinced me that we always have a choice. Not so much in what happens to us, but which response we choose. That enables me to handle everything in this life that I consider to be a dream [meaning: material reality is a dream, the other reality is real].

Her message is that there are alternatives, even if it seems we don't have any choices. For example, we can give in to our unhappiness and feel terribly sad about things we can't change—such as a sick body. But we can also choose a different emotion. The goal is then to choose an emotion that is an expression of love.

CHAPTER 11

The Way Back

In their NDEs, experiencers have been immersed in an alternate reality. After such a mind-boggling experience, returning to one's body and earthly life is no small feat. Sometimes NDErs are shocked by the announcement that they must go back. Often, they don't want to return, but the compulsion is so great that they must give in. There is no alternative. Sometimes they are interrupted in their wonderful experience by relatives on Earth who call them back. But occasionally they are given a choice: Stay here or go back. It is unclear why some NDErs have a choice and others don't.

As to the way back: Very often it happens so fast that NDErs have no words for it. However, in a fair number of cases, something interesting happens. For example, there is a loud noise, such as ringing or whistling. Frequently it is reported that everything feels much heavier, until they are completely subject to Earth's gravity.

And then there is the body they must return to: their own body, in which they have already lived for so many years. That body typically feels cold, dirty, and far too small. And once they are in it, it feels like a prison. Parking yourself back into your own body is no piece of cake.

————— YOU MUST GO BACK —————

Difficult Decision

For many NDErs, having to return to their physical bodies is a horrifying prospect. Rachel Finch felt this way. At the end of her NDE, she was asked if she would like to return to Earth.

> The absolute truth of my soul is that I felt completely insulted at this suggestion. I was horrified at the thought and felt myself loud within me, respond, "No!" There was a pause, and I felt a little confused, wondering why this was being asked of me. Again, the same question repeated within me, "Do you wish to go back?" Again, I said, "No."
>
> There was another pause and then I was shown the baby I had just birthed, lying in the crib beside my body. I was shown much from time to come. Various outcomes that depended solely on whether or not I returned to my body. There would be countless lives that would be touched with this Love if I returned and many that would not know it if I did not. I remember taking what can only be described as a deep, soul sigh. A knowing sigh. An understanding.
>
> Immediately after seeing this, and holding the vision of my newborn daughter in my "sight" and her possible future if I stayed, I said, "Yes." (Anonymous, 2019, June 10)

Crying Uncontrollably

In the midst of a blissful NDE, one of three angels suddenly said,

> "We have to go back." I said "No! This is so cool and I want to feel like this forever!" I pleaded with him, "I do not have any children, and I am not married. No one down there needs me!" I said, "The brain I have down there is

injured. I don't want to go back to that body. I'd like to stay here." I was told, "You will be made whole." . . . All of a sudden, I was in my mother's home, and I saw my Mom on the couch crying uncontrollably, which I had never seen before in my life. Then, in less than a second we were transported to my best friend's house, 10 miles away and I witnessed her shaking and crying violently, which I never witnessed. Apparently, this was a vision of the future had I been allowed to stay, and they would be mourning my death. So I told the angel, "Okay, okay, I'll go back." Instantaneously, I was back in my body. (Anonymous, 2012, January 3)

YOU MAY GO BACK

I Made My Choice

Anita Moorjani (2012) wrote a brilliant book about her NDE, which I recommend wholeheartedly. She also registered her experience with the IANDS archives. There she summarized a point in her NDE that she also had described in her book. I find it mind-bending, in that she learned that her intention would actually dictate what would happen in the material world. We normally think that once tests have been conducted, their results are already determined and merely await being analyzed and revealed. Anita learned that, instead, their results can change, depending on a deeper causality: one's own intentions.

I knew I was drifting in and out, between the two worlds, but every time I drifted into the other side, I was shown more and more scenes . . . Then I saw how my husband's purpose was linked to mine and how we had decided to come and experience this life together. If I died, he would probably follow soon after.

189

I was made to understand this during the tests of my organ functions. The results were not back yet. If I chose life, the results would show that my organs were functioning normally. If I chose death, the results would show organ failure as the cause of death due to cancer. I was able to change the outcome of the tests by my choice. I made my choice. As I started to wake up, in a very confused state, I could not at that time tell which side of the veil I was on. The doctors came rushing into the room with big smiles on their faces saying to my family "Good news, we got the results, and her organs are functioning. We can't believe it. Her body really did seem like it had shut down." (Anonymous, 2007, April 26)

Called by Many Names

During his entire NDE, this Jewish man sensed a very special person:

My Heart recognized HIM before my eyes did. I immediately walked over to him and asked, "Are You the Being, called JESUS," and with a warm soft, sense of Love and Laughter, he replied back, "I am called by many names, however because of your background you can call me BIG BROTHER, and I will call you, My Little Prince of Peace" . . . He then went on to indicate, that I could either stay with HIM or return to earth. However, if I did not return, many people would miss their connections, in order to complete their missions and purposes in life. (*Shalom G NDE*, n.d.)

—————————— GOING BACK ——————————

Gradually Getting Heavier

An Iranian man was hit by a car and taken to hospital in an ambulance. Once in the building, he discovered that while his body was being transferred down the corridors to the ICU, his transparent bodily form could effortlessly go through walls.

> It was like as I got close to a wall, it would go away. I could not feel any physical thing or barrier.

As he hovered just below the ceiling, he saw the doctors and nurses working on his body. They were trying to resuscitate him—tubes in his throat, cardiac massage, injections, electric shocks. At first it did not seem to work; he didn't feel anything. However, slowly he felt himself becoming heavier. He felt that there was a pull towards that body he saw on the table. Then finally, it worked.

> When I was entering my body, I heard a whistle and felt that I was in an open and dark space that was like a funnel and I was entering my body from the head. After I entered my body, I felt a lot of intense pain. I think I was out for 15 to 20 minutes. (*Arshan NDE*, 1996)

Weight on My Chest

After having had a tour through hellish situations, George Ritchie (2004) traveled through a huge void that felt full of promise. Then he saw a heavenly city in the distance made from the same light as the "Presence" who was with him. He was approaching it very rapidly. There were figures that seemed to detach themselves from that city, and they started approaching him at the speed of light. However, he suddenly felt that he was drawn back at an even greater speed. Walls were closing in around him, feeling narrow and box-like, and he recognized that they were the walls of the room in which his body lay. He saw this "lump-like thing," his body, and pleaded not to be left there.

> I felt consciousness slipping from me. My mind began to blur . . . My throat was on fire and the weight on my chest was crushing me. (p. 74)

He then opened his eyes and found himself back in his body again.

Falling Through Levels of Consciousness

Nicholas had his NDE after an accident at the gym. He found himself in an infinite dark void in which he could move freely. It felt good. His problems were gone. He called it the "highest plane of consciousness," and he had his life review. Suddenly he saw light coming from what looked like a door.

> As I approached the illuminated doorway, a thunderous male's voice echoed throughout the darkness and told me, "Nicholas, it is not your time." Immediately it felt as if I was lifted up and thrown backward. I literally felt like I "fell" through each level of consciousness until I reached this plane where my human body existed.
>
> Suddenly I opened my eyes to see that I was in a hospital bed and began crying hysterically. (Anonymous, 2012, June 20)

We're Always Here for You

Yolaine Stout (n.d.) had an NDE in which she met Jesus who told her not to waste her life thinking she was not loved. Then he slowly disappeared, and the room went dark again. She wanted to move, but it turned out that she was no longer in her body. That was a shock to her. Then her body pulled her back into it. It was like being pushed back into her body.

> It was extremely unpleasant. Out there I was light, but then I had to get into that dank, dense, cold body.

She likened it to when you fall back into a pool of cold mud that absorbs you. It was a shock to her. She kept trying to go back to that light, and in a brief moment where it came back a little bit, it was like it said: "We're always here for you. It's always here. Don't worry."

Mom Was Calling Out My Name

A Chinese woman unknowingly used chopsticks that had been used with fish, to which she was allergic. She suffered a reaction in which she was unable to breathe. At the hospital:

> That middle-aged, female doctor said, "We are losing her. Have her family come." As my Mom walked into the patient ward, she jumped onto the bed holding my body, rocking and calling my name out loud. The whole room was filled with her voice that could bring down the ceiling, and the doctors and the nurses had stepped aside.

Meanwhile, she was having a blissful NDE—which suddenly stopped:

> I began to fall down, and I screamed out loud, "I don't want to go back! I don't want to go back! I don't want to go back." But it was completely futile. The descending speed was the same as when I was ascending . . . Personally, I experienced my soul had given up and left my body, but because of Mom's strong will [my soul re-entered the flesh and I] came back alive at last. The forceful descent was due to Mom's persevering determination . . . If it was not for her crazy persistence calling out my name, I probably would have stayed in that other realm. (*Chenguan NDE*, n.d.)

Wake Up!

Tetty Pols-Visser (Pols-Visser & Oosterhof, 2010) described how, during her NDE:

> I know that I am on the doorstep and that heaven is stretched out before me. In front of me I see a road that leads to a big gate, bathing in radiant golden light. (p. 76)

She was beckoned to the gate by a male figure in a long brown cloak with a large hood that hid his face.

> And although I can't really see the expression on his face or in his eyes, his whole being radiates love and trust. I feel safe in his presence. I am being acknowledged. (p. 76)

She knew that if she approached the gate, the doors would open for her, and she could proceed into heaven. She also knew that she too could be with God. She was looking forward to entering. However, suddenly, far away, she could hear a voice shouting her name.

> That voice is not from the Light. I feel that it wants to pull me away from the Light. My whole being resists it. (p. 76)

Nevertheless, she was being pulled away from the Light. She struggled because she had planned to stay. The voice came closer. It was the voice of her husband, Koos.

> He wants to hold me back, but how can he do this to me to call me back? There I will never feel what I feel here. I don't want to hear Koos, I don't want to go back. But I can't resist the voice calling: "Tetty, Tetty, wake

up." Slowly I feel that I am being pulled away from the Light. The Light in me extinguishes. Heaven is hidden from my view as if an invisible hand is covering it with a dark veil. What remains is an emptiness and darkness. I start to cry. (p. 76)

To Calm the Doctor

In his unpublished interview with me, Bill Gladstone described how he was up against the ceiling looking down at the doctor who was trying to revive his lifeless body. He encountered loving beings who escorted him and took him away. He could still hear the distressed shouting of the doctor.

> I felt bathed by loving beings with whom I was connected. I did not recognize these beings who created a kind of light bubble around me. They were escorting me on a trip and I felt their love and comfort. It was only the distraction of the shouting of the doctor trying to get the attention of the lifeless body on the floor that stopped me from continuing the journey with these light beings . . . The doctor's concern was the lifeless body on the floor that would not respond to him. I had no emotion about what was occurring, but I realized that the lifeless body was my body, and I made the decision to re-enter the body so that the doctor would calm down. I had the sense the doctor was important and I wanted to prevent him from suffering. I had no thought of death or any fear of any kind.

———————— IT DOESN'T FIT ————————

Hugging

The way back usually goes so quickly that NDErs do not have time to fully experience it. But there are exceptions, especially when the return to the body seems difficult. After being struck by lightning and having her NDE, Elizabeth Krohn's sense of herself, her being, had expanded to such an extent that it had to be squeezed back into her body with some force and effort. The companion she met during her NDE told her that he could help her back into her body only by hugging her very tightly, "so tightly it would feel as if my bones were being crushed" (Krohn & Kripal, 2018, p. 32).

Big Expanse

Another NDEr described the process of re-embodiment similarly:

> So I had to squeeze my big expanse back into that tiny body that was, by now, half way outside that wrecked car. I couldn't fit very well. It took me 6 months to get comfortable. (Anonymous, 2016, September 23)

Parallel Parking

In spite of her resistance, Kimberly Clark Sharp (2003) returned to her body. In her book she wrote that she isn't very good at parallel parking and that she always ends up feet away from the curb. Likewise, she missed getting into her body by several feet, as well, and was able to have a look at herself from the side. She was astonished to see her body, for the first time, from an angle she had never seen before.

> I looked at my body, the body I knew so well, and was surprised by my detachment . . . Whatever constituted the self I knew as me was no longer there. My essence, my consciousness, my memories, my personality were outside, not in, that person of flesh. (pp. 26–27)

Then she saw a man trying to resuscitate her. He leaned over her to "put his mouth to mine." Through his touch, she was able to enter her body again. But his touch made her observe and experience what was happening to her and that total stranger.

> I realized I knew everything about him emotionally. I could feel his nervousness and even his discomfort about performing this intimate, humane service in front of a gawking crowd. But it was his compassion, his love for me, a total stranger, that guided me . . . back into my body. (p. 27)

Such Heaviness

Carol Lynn Vengroff (2012) was given to understand that she couldn't stay in that wonderful environment of her NDE. She was sent on a mission to Earth, and that mission was "planted in my heart." When the moment came that she had to return, she wondered how this would be possible.

> I . . . was wondering how they were going to condense and fit my cosmos-expanded light-being of joy, love, and contentment, that was now me, back into that tiny, microscopic speck of a particle that was my twelve-year-old human body, lying in a bed somewhere. . . .
>
> In what seemed like an instant, I was catapulted, sucked and drawn back into my body, and pulled in by an overpowering magnetic and gravitational force.
>
> Suddenly, I felt weighed down with such heaviness that I was positive it would suffocate and paralyze me. My spirit, my essence, and my physical body were united once again. (pp. 43–44)

Coca-Cola Can

Ellyn Dye (2023) refused to go back to her body, and "loving Beings" told her that her decision was fine: It was her choice. The last thing she could remember was that they said they would show her what she could accomplish if she chose to go back.

The next moment she woke up in the emergency room of a hospital. Shocked, she knew she had somehow changed her mind and agreed to come back to her body, but she couldn't remember why. She exclaimed aloud, "Why am I here?" A nearby nurse didn't understand what she meant and told her she was in the hospital because of a car accident.

Ellyn did not sustain any serious injuries from the collision. She did not understand how she ended up in her body again. She said:

> I could not understand how that giant, expansive Self that I AM had jammed itself back into this small body, like trying to shove an elephant into a Coca-Cola can!

PRISON

Solid Structure

Tienke Klein (2006) described her return from her NDE:

> That was so painful, both mentally and physically. While going lower and lower, the love was gradually leaving and was replaced by more structures, until, with a bang!, I fell in my body again. And that, of course, is a solid structure. (Klein, 2008)

Abrupt Return

Lee Thornton (2014) felt like she was very far from Earth during her NDE. In her book she wrote that she felt as if she had landed in another galaxy, a long distance from our Milky Way. Her out-of-body journey to that place seemed to have taken place gradually: from the hospital ceiling into and through the atmosphere into a black, star-filled sky from which location she could see the Earth, and past many stars to an enormous dark void. In comparison, her return journey was very short and abrupt:

> The next thing I knew I was back in my body. Unlike the long journey into reaches beyond, my return to earth was abrupt, like the shock of birth. (pp. 99–100)

After she had arrived back in her body, it felt extremely restrictive, especially compared to the enormous freedom she had experienced just before. She felt like being a "prisoner returned to her cell" (p. 100).

Trapped in Bad Meat

This child had been ill with fever and became unconscious. She was drawn back to Earth owing to the distress that her condition had caused to her family. Once she had decided to enter her body, she felt horrible:

> I felt terrible: heavy, sore, chilled, and extremely sad. I felt as if I was trapped in a large piece of bad meat. I could see out of my eye sockets as if I were wearing a mask and I felt physically burdened by, and separate from, my body. I was well aware of being a separate entity from the body that I was inhabiting. (Anonymous, 2013, July 19)

Monument in Patience

This NDEr (Anonymous, 2006, April 17) was impressed by the magnificence, power, and greatness of the Light. She said that the Light was not human but, rather, "took a mild resemblance to a human" to make her feel at ease. She also said that this Light was a kind of "gatekeeper" and had informed her that she could not stay. With great patience the Light told her repeatedly that she had to go back. There was no "anger or frustration" on its part. She said:

> He was a monument in patience. He was a pillar of love. But he was strict with me by refusing to let me stay there, like a father forcing his kid to go to the first day of school despite its tantrums and crying.

Once she had accepted her fate to return to her body, things happened incredibly fast:

> I felt myself literally fall into my body and remember seeing my body on the bed right before I fell back into it. I was so exhilarated and delighted at my experience, and so angry at the same time to be back in this restricted, limited, difficult plane of existence.

She mentioned that she easily gets "irritated" and "frustrated" that she must live again in a body. She calls her body "a prison (sad, but true)."

Small Price
This NDEr described the return into the body as:

> both startling and insightful. As I . . . re-entered my body, I came to the total realization that it is actually very uncomfortable to "live" in a body. A side effect of experiencing this kind of life. I immediately experienced a kind of ache. As though I was being encased in a shell that was just the tiniest amount too small. Not painful, but, definitely noticeable. And definitely caused a kind of ache.

But, immediately after feeling the "ache" and letting go of the shock that came with it, came the realization that it is just an acceptable, albeit uncomfortable, part of this existence. And it tells you in an odd sort of way, that all the aches and pains in life truly are nothing compared to what great and unimaginable joy and warmth you can draw from life. That those aches and pains are a small price to pay. That it is, in the end, all worth it.

Then, reminiscent of Nancy Rynes, whose NDE excerpt opened Chapter 10, this NDEr concluded that we must trust that, before we were born, we had decided we wanted this kind of life, even if we cannot remember why we chose it (Anonymous, 2003, November 28, 10:36 AM).

CHAPTER 12

Aftereffects

For most NDErs, the experience is profound, and virtually every experiencer is changed—in many cases, completely transformed. For nearly all experiencers, there is a distinct difference between life before and after the NDE. It may also take years before the NDEr has fully integrated the experience into their life. It is not just because on Earth they can't find the freedom and unconditional love they had experienced in that *other world*. It is more than that: They realize and understand that money, power, and status are not important—that far more important is their contact with other people, animals, and nature. After all, they have seen and felt that we are all very closely connected—in fact, one with all existence.

Sometimes the feeling of separation from that other world is so strong that they don't really want to be on Earth anymore. The separation hurts. It hurts a lot. In fact, they suffer severe homesickness.

The changes in NDErs affect not only the NDErs themselves but also their loved ones and others who are close to them. Others often no longer recognize the NDEr, and frequently, as a result, friendships shift, organizational affiliations change, careers take a completely different direction, and marriages end.

The aftereffects of NDEs are diverse, but bear in mind that not every NDEr displays all of them. Some of them have already been mentioned, such as reduced self-interest and increased desire to be of service to other people and to nature. Depression has also been mentioned.

Perhaps the most frequently reported and important aftereffect is that NDErs generally no longer have a fear of death. It is also striking that NDErs become much more sensitive. Sound and light can easily become overwhelming, leading some NDErs to avoid large crowds. They may need less medication to have the same effect. NDErs' psychic and mediumship qualities often increase, too. That is because the door to the other side of life hasn't entirely shut. Although the crack is not large enough to return to that beautiful place, it is sufficiently large to keep in touch with it. Sometimes this connection increases their healing potential. This chapter gives some extraordinary examples of self-healing.

It is also striking that NDErs generally become less religious but much more spiritual. And then there are some very strange aftereffects, such as interference with electronic devices and electrical appliances.

NO FEAR OF DEATH

Another Dimension

The other very important effect of the NDE was that it changed my view of death and the afterlife, taking away my fear of the unknown regarding what happens after we die. It convinced me that life does not cease to exist when the body dies; that we have a soul that is connected to a greater consciousness that continues to live in spirit form in another dimension . . . a realm where a higher intelligence of unconditional love exists. (Anonymous [Lee Thornton], 2013, June 17)

More Tolerance

Since that experience, my mind and soul are more important for me than my body. Some say that I have a healing effect on them. Now I feel I get along better with people and have more tolerance for them. I can better understand their feelings and what is going on inside them. This experience has changed my life and my thinking. I am no longer afraid of dying, as I have experienced it once. (*Arshan NDE, 1996*)

NATURE AND OTHER PEOPLE

Vastly More Complex

As a result of my experience, my understanding of the nature of the universe has changed entirely. It's now clear to me that the physical world we experience is part of something vastly more complex with facets that I never before would have believed possible. I became far more interested in being in nature and more interested in talking to and connecting with other people. (Anonymous, 2020, April 19)

People's Emotions

Ever since then it's like I have a heightened awareness of people's emotions, or I feel the impact of how others are feeling more profoundly. (Anonymous, 2006, April 17)

Animals Follow Me Home

This childhood NDEr (Anonymous, 2013, July 19) reported that she has "very unique and close relationships with animals." She also said that on one occasion she had "been asked to leave the zoo because all of the animals I passed came over to stand in front of me in their enclosures. Many pressed themselves right up against the bars or glass and tried to touch me."

NDErs often report that people are drawn to them for no particular reason—and that even strangers approach the NDEr. That was the case with this childhood NDEr:

> People and animals have even followed me home for no discernible reason other than to be with me. I have grown used to this behavior and I no longer question it. I also appear to have a VERY green thumb and plants that florists have declared as dead come to life for me. I just seem to know intuitively what to do. (Anonymous, 2013, July 19)

The NOW

In my unpublished interview with Johan Verhage, he told me that he had his NDE while battling severe pneumonia. He was at home in bed when, at one point, he could no longer breathe. He was shocked but didn't panic. He sank quietly into unconsciousness. Suddenly he felt his soul and energy detach themselves from his body, and immediately afterwards he found himself in a tunnel with a bright light blue-white light at the end, to which he felt strongly attracted. He said that it emitted a love and serenity that we do not know on Earth.

> In the distance I saw two shadows standing in front of the light. When I got closer, I saw that they were my deceased grandpa and grandma. Happy to see me, grandma spread her arms out to me with a blissful smile as if to say, "come here." But just before the reunion my grandpa jumped in front of me and with a stern, penetrating look, an outstretched arm and a wagging finger he pointed me back. No words were spoken, [but the

message was clear]: "Back-up, you're not done yet and still have things to work out on Earth!"

Johan's NDE had a limited number of components, such as an out-of-body experience, a feeling of bliss, a tunnel, and deceased relatives. Among the absent components were a substantial conversation, a life review, and visions of the world beyond the tunnel. Nevertheless, this NDE had a huge impact on Johan. An NDE does not have to be at all deep to leave a profound, lasting, and even life-changing impression on the NDEr.

Johan said that a lot has changed in his life and that it feels as if he was "born again." He sees the world through different eyes. For example, material things are less important to him; he tries to become more loving and to treat everyone with more respect. He has started to live more from his feelings instead of from his mind. He is living in the "NOW," written in capital letters.

He found that people who are disinterested in spirituality don't understand him well. At the same time, he discovered that because of his enormous inner growth, he has met entirely different people with whom he resonates in ways he would not have prior to his NDE.

DEPRESSED

Desire to Be Home

Returning into one's body after an NDE and adapting to a life without the total love of the Light is extremely difficult for many NDErs. Some even consider suicide to be able to return, as was the case with Rachel Finch. But fortunately for both them and us, they manage to come through this very difficult period.

It took my spirit longer to recover than my body, though that in itself was a long time. I was very depressed, for many years, and often dealt with suicidal thoughts because the desire to be "home" was so great. I was confused for the longest time. I was afraid. I found being in a body painful, restricting, and limiting. I am still greatly uncomfortable with it; however, I have learnt to love and be grateful for my life and breath . . . I have never forgotten a single moment of [my experience] and doubt I ever will. It took me time, but I allowed it to transform me in the most beautiful of ways, and I try every day to live and love the way I was loved in those very sacred moments. (Anonymous, 2019, June 10)

Rachel described the pain she had in processing her return to Earth in verse:

The time I spend
recovering, is
misshapen.
I am a lamb in lion form,
I am supernova caged.
I am a mist, bodied and
shackled, ready to
shed this skin and every
layer peels back a new
unknowing.
(Finch, 2019, p. 78)

Every Hour or Even More Than That

Christina, who survived a kidnapping and near drowning when she was eight years old, manifested several NDE aftereffects. Immediately after being resuscitated by her father, she felt deeply depressed, almost suicidal. That was because she came back to Earth from a place she called "home." She told me that she still thinks about her NDE every day and often several times a day. Other aftereffects included skills she gained, such as telepathy, seeing auras, and the ability to heal people (Anonymous, 2012, November 18).

——PSYCHIC AND MEDIUMSHIP ABILITIES——

Seeing Spirits

Christina is not alone in having gained psychic abilities following her NDE. Jane Bannister also reported such ability, though in her case it was temporary:

> This experience left me with a strange psychic ability where for about six months I was almost constantly clairvoyant and seeing spirit guides. It was as if the barrier between the two worlds had been opened and not closed. (Anonymous, 2010, December 20, 16:40)

Accident on a Highway

After Catja de Rijk (2021) had her NDE, she discovered that more had changed than only her view of the world, her friendships, and nature. She discovered that she, too, had become psychic. She could "see" things that other people couldn't see. In her book, she gave several examples.

One Sunday she felt that there would be a car accident that day on a specific highway in the center of the Netherlands. When the accident did actually happen, it had a big impact on her for two reasons.

Of course, the first reason was that it was a very serious accident with three fatalities, including the death of a well-known Dutch actor. The second reason was that it gave her clear evidence that she had psychic abilities and could see into the future.

Later, there were other examples of "seeing" into the future, including the terrorist attack in Brussels in March 2016. Fortunately, she not only could see these kinds of serious events, but she also could provide helpful personal information, such as telling someone precisely where, in a large shed full of junk, they could find the deeds of ownership of a small airplane (pp. 109–122).

Plane Crash on the Hudson River

Some remarkable aftereffects are described in Elizabeth Krohn and Jeffrey Kripal's (2018, pp. 83–93) book, *Changed in a Flash*. After being struck by lightning, Elizabeth had an extensive NDE. In earthly time she had been unconscious for only a few minutes, but she felt she had stayed in that other world for two weeks.

Some of the aftereffects she wrote about are experienced by many NDErs. For example, she experienced electrical interference—in which electrical equipment, such as watches, cell phones, and computers, malfunction in the vicinity of the NDEr, especially when they are emotionally aroused. But more amazing were the predictive dreams she experienced on a regular basis.

Many of them are well documented. Initially that was not the case. She discovered that no one believed her when she had predictive dreams, because the time of the dream could not be ascertained precisely. Therefore, immediately after a predictive dream, she would write herself an e-mail describing all the details. When the e-mail was sent, it was automatically time-stamped, so that she had proof that she already knew the facts in advance.

In her book she gave some examples. She sent herself an e-mail in January 2009 with information about a plane crash in the Hudson River in New York in which she saw all the passengers standing on the wings of the floating aircraft. The time on the e-mail was more than 7 hours before a United Airlines plane flew through a flock of geese and had to make an emergency landing on the river.

She also described how, in March 2011, she saw an earthquake in Japan and an ensuing tsunami that destroyed the nuclear power plant in Fukushima.

The special thing about these predictive dreams is that she has apparently retained her ability from the NDE to see through time. Apparently, the door to the other side is still ajar, and Elizabeth can continue to look through the crack. Although other NDErs have also reported this aftereffect of being able to see through time into the future, Elizabeth's case, which involved highly specific predictive dreams, was new to me.

Tender Spots

Another NDEr who reported psychic aftereffects was Dannion Brinkley (2008, pp. 117–132) who, like Elizabeth Krohn, had his NDE after being struck by lightning. After his NDE he discovered that he could read people's minds. And later he discovered that when he touched people, he could see what he calls a "home movie" with images of their home situation. He might witness arguments between family members or colleagues, or see the suffering experienced by the person he had touched. Sometimes when he picked up an object belonging to someone else, he saw their life circumstances or the history of the object itself.

Among the examples he provided in his book was mindreading. During a business meeting with Norwegians, he understood what they were talking about in their own language—although he did not speak Norwegian. An example of a "home movie" was when he made a deal with a man who bought a car from him. The moment they made the deal and shook hands, Dannion was shown the buyer's home situation: His children were forcing him to sell his house and give them the proceeds.

These kinds of psychic aftereffects, this psychic ability, are not limited to people who were struck by lightning. They happen to many NDErs to a greater or lesser extent.

When NDErs have no control over this psychic ability, they find this trait quite annoying. In fact, Dannion confessed this when he admitted that he has been given access to "a person's most tender spots, the areas of his life that are most shielded from public view" (p. 128).

Although he sometimes sees his gift as a burden, the conclusion of his story must be that it also has enabled him to help many people. This also applies to the many other NDErs who have similar gifts.

Yellow Bubbles

Holden, Foster, and Kinsey (2014) have researched so-called *spontaneous mediumship experiences* in which, after their NDE, an NDEr psychically experiences an uninvited visit by a deceased person asking the NDEr to convey a message to another living person. The authors found that at least some NDErs who never had such visits prior to their NDE *did* have them afterwards. In their article, they provided several interesting examples.

In one example, an NDEr was on the phone with her sister, whose husband had passed away (*Romona B NDE*). Suddenly her field of vision turned yellow, "like someone put a yellow sheet of paper in front of my eyes," and then it returned to normal colors but was filled with bubbles. This happened over and over, and then she heard a voice saying repeatedly, "Tell her, tell her." The voice was so loud that she finally gave in and told her sister what she was seeing: yellow bubbles. The sister reacted extremely happily, because "yellow bubbles" was her deceased husband's and her secret password. Before his passing, they had made a pact that, as proof of an afterlife, whoever died first would find a way to convey the password to the surviving partner.

SELF-HEALING

Redirect Blood Flow

Some NDErs have the ability to heal others or themselves. One NDEr (Anonymous, 2004, March 25, 9:14 PM) had three broken ribs and bruised kidneys, spleen, and liver. He was bleeding internally, and the doctors weren't sure where. He said he was going to consciously heal himself. He could feel exactly what was wrong with his body and where.

> I could redirect blood flow and nutrients to areas that needed it and away from areas that were bleeding. I could will my flesh and bones to grow back together. When I had a CT scan, the technicians ran another because the readings were so strange. There was no brain damage whatsoever, which was considered impossible given the extent of my injuries and how long my brain had been without oxygen while I was clinically dead.

He woke up in the middle of the night and realized that his doctor was sitting in a chair in his room. He was surprised and thought the doctor was sitting there showing concern. That is why he told the doctor that he was doing well and that the doctor would do better taking care of someone else who needed him more. The doctor replied:

> "I know, but what's happening to you is unbelievable. You should be dead. I can't turn my back on a miracle. God is allowing me the opportunity to witness this, and

I just can't walk away." I later found out that his daughter had been in a car accident and had similar injuries.
He had been questioning God, and he thought what
was happening to me before his eyes was God's answer
that He was still here.

Who Would Look After My Son?

Noël de Waele was in a particularly difficult situation (Coppes,
2021/2022). His marriage had virtually died. His wife was
often away, sometimes for days and weeks at a time, with
no one knowing where she was. On one occasion she had
taken the car along with the savings for their son Maurice's
education. She also had severe mood swings—probably due
to a borderline personality disorder. Consequently, he was
in a constant state of great tension, and despite being almost
alone in caring for their 12-year-old son, he was terrified that
his wife or in-laws would try to get custody of Maurice and
take him away.

Years of stress took their toll. At one point, his health had
eroded to such an extent that every morning he had great
difficulty getting his body to move and get out of bed. He
looked like an old man instead of a young father.

He went to the doctor, who tested Noël's blood. A few
days later, the doctor came to his home with the results. The
blood values were so poor that he said, "I'm amazed you're
still alive." He wanted to call an ambulance straightaway
and have Noël hospitalized immediately. But Noël resisted
strongly: "Who will take care of my son then?"

The doctor prescribed a certain medication and said that
if Noël didn't feel better after the weekend, he really had to
go to the hospital.

Due to his psychological and physical crisis, that weekend
Noël had his NDE. In his NDE, he met his late sister who told
him he couldn't stay because he had a task to do. She also

told him that he would be fine and that he should not worry, because Maurice would stay with him.

When he came to, he was extremely happy. He felt he had to change, and it gave him a kickstart. While he was still in bed, he felt himself getting better. And when he tried to get up, he noticed that it was no problem at all. He felt born again. He had his energy back. It was because of the reassuring message and his task. He didn't really know what that task was, but he certainly had one. That also gave him the energy to continue.

Although he had not touched the medicine, after the weekend he called the doctor and told him that he didn't need to take further action because the medicine had taken effect. He knew his sister's message was true and that he was better. And, indeed, his son was not taken away from him.

Doctors Ran Tests Over and Over

After Anita Moorjani (2012) had spoken to her deceased father during her NDE, she arrived at a border. Her father said that if she were to cross it, she could not come back to Earth. She saw the consequences of her choice if she were to decide to do so—such as deep sadness in her family.

She understood either decision was okay. She could either cross the border or go back. She understood that if she went back, her body would soon recover from the cancer, because her body would adjust to her inner state that had been changed by the NDE.

She chose to go back. From that moment on there was a miraculous and rapid healing of her body. Within two days she was able to eat independently, within three days the tumors had clearly shrunk, and after five days she was able to leave the ICU.

During a presentation for IANDS (Moorjani, n.d.), she said the doctors were so amazed that they ran tests over and over again, because they didn't believe what they saw. It was as if they were doing tests hoping that they might still find cancer somewhere.

HEALING OTHERS

Whereas some NDErs report having themselves been healed *during* their NDE, many NDErs have developed the ability to heal others *following* their NDE. Take the example of Anna Best, with whom I conducted an unpublished interview. The first major change she noticed after her NDE was that she was no longer afraid of death. Her sense of God also became universal; she said that "the walls of the church started to oppress me."

She also said that her innate sensitivity became stronger and stronger. However, she reported, "because I didn't know what to do with it, I got busy with all kinds of earthly matters. Raising the children also took up a lot of time and attention."

Yet she could not continue denying her raised sensitivity. After many health problems, the right people crossed her path—people who encouraged her to stop denying her open connection to the other side of life. She trained as a psychic healer and has since treated many people successfully. About this ability, she said:

> While treating people, I experience that when I attune myself to the person, I find myself on a different level of consciousness. I tune into the Light and then I am in the Light. The Cosmic, Divine Light—that envelops and protects everyone, and that helps people to get rid of limiting emotions and blockages to heal on a soul level—helps me to do my "work" . . . I feel lucky to know myself surrounded by this Divine, healing Light and to experience that on this Earth I am connected in love with all living beings and everything that grows and blossoms.

ELECTRICITY

Microwave

Elizabeth Krohn's (Krohn & Kripal, 2018) predictive dreams are described just above, but her other aftereffects are just as remarkable. Like other NDErs with electromagnetic aftereffects, Elizabeth cannot wear battery-powered watches, because the batteries die almost immediately and the watches stop. Lights sometimes blow when she walks past, and iPhone earplugs are always very painful. She also hates the microwave. (p. 98)

Streetlights Go Out

One of the NDErs in Liz Dale's (2008) book reported:

> Coming out of the hospital, every sound was unbearably loud. Daylight, even when overcast or cloudy, was blinding and it actually hurt my eyes. Even now, years later, I can't stand bright lights at home, in supermarkets, or stores. I couldn't speak for over two weeks after I left the hospital. I had great difficulty walking, writing, eating and sleeping. I couldn't stand television, violence, radios, or movies. I had constant feelings of care and love . . . At times, I feel as if a jolt or bolt of lightning is passing through me in a flash. For over two years, whenever I wore a watch, it would stop running . . . If I walked under a streetlight, it would go out. The kids would beg me to run from one end of the street to the other—they knew if I did, each streetlight would go out as I ran under them. If I came near a computer, it would goof up or stop working . . . Everything and everyone became precious to me. All fear left me. (pp. 119–120)

───── LESS RELIGIOUS, MORE SPIRITUAL ─────

Not the Endpoint

After their experience, although some NDErs remain involved or even become more involved in organized religion, most NDErs move away from the religion of their upbringing. Sometimes they become interested in what other religions have to say without committing themselves to any organized religion. Their view of religion is broadened. In fact, you can say that after their experience they usually become less religious but more spiritual. This was the case for a 14-year-old boy who had his NDE during his near-drowning experience at a Boy Scout camp. He had been raised Catholic and attended a school where they prepared boys to become priests.

> Religion, any religion, didn't matter to me anymore. I no longer saw the church as the endpoint but rather as a vehicle some people use to the endpoint. (Anonymous, 2004, March 4, 8:58 PM)

No Monopoly on Heaven

A Muslim NDEr said that

> Allah (God) has given man many roads to get to him, and none has a monopoly on Heaven.

He also said that

> I have changed slowly over the years since [my NDE]. I'm more carefree, forgiving, and humbler, and I love diversity. (*Caan S NDE*, n.d.)

———— EXCEPTIONAL TALENTS ————

Rocker, Not a Piano Lover

After their experience, some NDErs develop new abilities, such as becoming artistic or starting to have a green thumb. However, there are also reports of some very exceptional talents.

Tony Cicoria (n.d.), orthopedic surgeon and motorcycle lover, was one day outdoors on a payphone with his mother, when he was struck by lightning. In his NDE, he encountered a wonderful bright light and felt absolute peace. When he started to enjoy where he was, he suddenly was back, not in his body yet, but close to it. He noticed someone performing CPR on him and asked her to stop—which, of course, she could not hear. He pleaded with God or "whoever was on that other side" to let him stay. But he survived.

Although he had never in his life been interested in piano music—he had always been a rocker rather than a piano-lover—several weeks after his NDE, he felt an urgent desire to hear classical piano. He gave into the urge and bought some piano recordings. Then, by coincidence—or some might say synchronicity—one of his babysitters needed a place to store a piano. That really got him going. He bought some books on how to play the piano, and playing became an obsession. He then took lessons and practiced for many hours—sometimes six hours a day—and became very good at it. Eventually, he started to write piano music himself and has now written and performed several major works, such as his *Lightning Sonata*. He thinks that this music is the reason why he was allowed to come back to earthly life (Cicoria, n.d.).

Quantum Theory

At age 33, Tom Sawyer was a mechanic and was under his pickup truck working to repair it. When the truck fell off the jacks, it crushed his chest, pushing all the air out of his lungs. He had his NDE, feeling very much awake, having no sense of time, and traveling at the speed of light through a tunnel to infinity. The light that he encountered was more perfect than anything he had ever known. This unconditional loving Light conveyed some important messages to Tom. It contained all knowledge, and he understood that any question he asked would be answered instantaneously. So, he asked many questions. He had a complete life review in which he experienced everything he did from the standpoint of all the people he had interacted with. He learned that there was no such thing as hell, and the God he experienced was a truly loving God. He got the choice to either stay and be part of the Light or go back to his earthly life. He understood that if he stayed, he would "cease to function normally, I would no longer be exactly myself, that I would be an actual integral part of the Light . . . I would be light" (Sawyer, n.d.).

Although his NDE was interesting in itself, afterwards he discovered that he had retained bits and pieces of information. Important physicists were on his mind: Max Planck, Niels Bohr, and Albert Einstein. He started to have a great interest in physics, and he wrote down his thoughts. When he found a book about Max Planck, the originator of quantum theory, he found some of the equations that he himself had previously written down.

OTHER AFTEREFFECTS

Math Problems
It was in the middle of the summer in a hot car without air-conditioning. This young nine-year-old girl was on a road trip with her parents when she had a fit and stopped breathing. Then she found herself in a cave-like place. She was not standing on the ground but was floating. It was so awkward

that the young girl became confused, frightened, and very worried. It all ended well when she saw a bright light. She had to return to her body.

After a few months she became aware of sounds and voices in her head. She said:

> I don't know who it was, but it was helping me in my math problems at school. The sounds didn't allow me to sleep at night. I was so scared, and no one ever believed me. I begged the voice to stop talking, and it did. Now I regret that, but now it's too late. (*Samieh NDE*, n.d.)

Schoolyard

Apart from recounting his miraculous healing, Noël de Waele described other aftereffects:

> I can no longer handle crowds, yelling and too many people around me. For example, I never walk past a schoolyard during playtime. My judgment has also changed. I observe and no longer judge, because I know that there is always a reason why people do what they do. (Coppes, 2021/2022, p. 25)

CHAPTER 13

Conclusion

Hopefully all the quotes together have given you a fair impression of NDEs. My intention was to let them be like brushstrokes in an impressionist painting. I leave it up to you to form your own picture and to enjoy it. And I really hope you do, because based on all the quotes, I have created for myself a wonderful picture of our world and of our afterlife, and I do enjoy the sight of it.

What do the quotes mean to me? In essence, the preliminary conclusion I arrived at after so many years of meetings with NDErs, reading about their experiences, and studying them, is brief:

There is a large, growing number of these extraordinary experiences, and most of them have had a profound impact on the people who have had such an experience. So, there must be something in them. They cannot simply be ignored.

What is remarkable is that a subset of these NDEs consists of so-called veridical observations. They are observations that NDErs made and that were subsequently independently verified—observations NDErs could have made only if their consciousness was actually outside their bodies. Like the number of NDEs, the number of these veridical observations is growing quickly. They seem to give circumstantial evidence that our consciousness can exist separate from our body. If such is the case, then we may conclude that NDEs are not only extraordinary, but that they are also real, and if so, then humanity needs to heed their important messages. In my opinion, there are two such messages.

The first is that Love is the most important thing there is, and that Unconditional Love awaits us when our body dies and our consciousness is released. That Unconditional Love seems to take the form of Light mentioned so often in NDEs. This Love and Light is unconditional, and it is there for everyone. No exceptions, not one single one: Otherwise, it wouldn't be unconditional.

The second message is that we are very thoroughly interconnected with each other, with other animals, with nature, and in fact with all that exists, even rocks and stones. However, if we take a closer look at what many NDErs are saying, the conclusion could be more extreme than just this interconnectedness. It should probably be that, seen from another dimension, we are all ONE. Love is what seems to bind us, and the purest and most perfect love and light is what we all have within us: the divine Love and Light. What we need to do is express this divinity that is within all of us.

I believe that if enough people are aware that all is thoroughly connected and that love is the most important thing, humanity could really take the next step. A kind of heaven on Earth will then be within our reach.

It seems only fitting that I give the last word of this impressionist work to an NDEr:

The overwhelming sense I got . . . were messages of joy/ elation that . . . everything would be okay for everyone in the world. (Anonymous, 2020, April 19)

References

An online version of this list is available at
https://iands.org/impressions-references.

Alexander, E., III. (2012). *Proof of heaven: A neurosurgeon's journey into the afterlife.* Simon & Schuster.

Alexander, E. (n.d.). *My experience in coma.* Author. http://ebenalexander.com/about/my-experience-in-coma/

Anonymous. (2002, February 5, 1:18 PM). *[Untitled].* International Association for Near-Death Studies. https://iands.org/research/nde-research/nde-archives31/newest-accounts/630-archive-through-february-26-2002.html

Anonymous. (2003, November 11, 4:39 PM). *[Untitled].* International Association for Near-Death Studies. https://iands.org/research/nde-research/nde-archives31/newest-accounts/641-archive-through-december-5-2003.html

Anonymous. (2003, November 28, 10:36 AM). *[Untitled].* International Association for Near-Death Studies. https://iands.org/research/nde-research/nde-archives31/newest-accounts/641-archive-through-december-5-2003.html

Anonymous. (2004, March 4, 8:58 PM). *[Untitled].* International Association for Near-Death Studies. https://iands.org/research/nde-research/nde-archives31/newest-accounts/642-archive-through-march-11-2004.html

Anonymous. (2004, March 4, 9:06 PM). *[Untitled].* International Association for Near-Death Studies. https://iands.org/research/nde-research/nde-archives31/newest-accounts/642-archive-through-march-11-2004.html

Anonymous. (2004, March 25, 9:14 PM). *[Untitled]*. International Association for Near-Death Studies. https://iands.org/research/nde-research/nde-archives31/newest-accounts/643-archive-through-march-30-2004.html

Anonymous. (2004, March 30, 9:55 PM). *[Untitled]*. International Association for Near-Death Studies. https://iands.org/research/nde-research/nde-archives31/newest-accounts/644-archive-through-april-6-2004.html

Anonymous. (2006, January 30). *Three accounts*. International Association for Near-Death Studies. https://iands.org/research/nde-research/nde-archives31/newest-accounts/27-three-accounts.html

Anonymous. (2006, April 17). *Gargantuan energy source.* International Association for Near-Death Studies. https://iands.org/research/nde-research/nde-archives31/newest-accounts/66-gargantuan-energy-source.html

Anonymous. (2006, June 19). *Shimmering river of life.* International Association for Near-Death Studies. https://iands.org/ndes/nde-stories/iands-nde-accounts/85-shimmering-river-of-life.html

Anonymous. (2007, April 26). *Shown how an illness starts at an energetic level.* International Association for Near-Death Studies. https://iands.org/ndes/nde-stories/iands-nde-accounts/345-shown-how-illnesses-start-on-an-energetic-level.html

Anonymous. (2008, August 29). *Guided to do out of love.* International Association for Near-Death Studies. https://iands.org/ndes/nde-stories/iands-nde-accounts/488-guided-to-do-out-of-love.html

Anonymous. (2009, April 18). *All is everything, everything is one.* International Association for Near-Death Studies. https://iands.org/ndes/nde-stories/iands-nde-accounts/543-all-is-everything-everything-is-one.html

Anonymous. (2010, December 20, 17:04). *Velvety dark stillness.* International Association for Near-Death Studies.

https://iands.org/research/nde-research/nde-archives31/ newest-accounts/677-velvety-dark-stillness.html

Anonymous. (2010, December 20, 16:33). *The essence of life.* International Association for Near-Death Studies. https://iands.org/ndes/nde-stories/iands-nde-accounts/660 -the-essence-of-life.html

Anonymous. (2010, December 20, 16:40). *Superimposed.* International Association for Near-Death Studies. https:// iands.org/ndes/nde-stories/iands-nde-accounts/664 -superimposed.html

Anonymous. (2010, December 20, 16:48). *God exists.* International Association for Near-Death Studies. https://iands .org/ndes/nde-stories/iands-nde-accounts/669-god-exists .html

Anonymous. (2011, May 11). *Never wanted to leave the presence.* International Association for Near-Death Studies. https://iands.org/ndes/nde-stories/iands-nde-accounts/ 736-never-wanted-to-leave-the-presence.html

Anonymous. (2012, January 3). *Kissed by a marshmallow.* International Association for Near-Death Studies. https:// iands.org/ndes/nde-stories/iands-nde-accounts/809-kissed -by-a-marshmallow.html

Anonymous. (2012, June 20). *In the highest plain.* International Association for Near-Death Studies. https://iands .org/ndes/nde-stories/iands-nde-accounts/851-in-the -highest-plain.html

Anonymous. (2012, July 10). *Glorious light enveloping my soul.* International Association for Near-Death Studies. https://iands.org/ndes/nde-stories/iands-nde-accounts/855 -glorious-light-enveloping-my-soul.html

Anonymous. (2012, July 21). *There is no hell. We all go home.* International Association for Near-Death Studies. https://iands.org/ndes/nde-stories/iands-nde-accounts/858 -there-is-no-hell-we-all-go-home.html

References

Anonymous. (2012, September 1). *Revelation and transformation.* International Association for Near-Death Studies. https://iands.org/ndes/nde-stories/iands-nde-accounts/877 -revelation-and-transformation.html

Anonymous. (2012, November 18). *Unlimited peace and serenity.* International Association for Near-Death Studies. https://iands.org/ndes/nde-stories/iands-nde-accounts/ 894-unlimited-peace-and-serenity.html

Anonymous. (2013, April 17). *My awakening with the angels.* International Association for Near-Death Studies. https://iands.org/ndes/nde-stories/iands-nde-accounts/922 -my-awakening-with-the-angels.html

Anonymous. (2013, April 30). *Wheel of life.* International Association for Near-Death Studies. https://iands.org/ndes/ nde-stories/iands-nde-accounts/926-wheel-of-life.html

Anonymous. (2013, June 17). *My son, my Light.* International Association for Near-Death Studies. https://iands .org/ndes/nde-stories/iands-nde-accounts/939-my-son-my -light.html

Anonymous. (2013, July 19). *When I was 3 (58 years ago).* International Association for Near-Death Studies. https:// iands.org/ndes/nde-stories/iands-nde-accounts/963-when -i-was-3-58-years-ago.html

Anonymous. (2015, April 25). *Light always around us.* International Association for Near-Death Studies. https://iands .org/ndes/nde-stories/nde-like-accounts/452-light-always -around-us.html

Anonymous. (2016, September 23). *Sixty years in heaven, thirty minutes Earth time.* International Association for Near-Death Studies. https://iands.org/ndes/nde-stories/iands -nde-accounts/1165-sixty-years-in-heaven-thirty-minutes -earth-time.html

Anonymous. (2017, February 17). *It is here in our bodies that the lessons of love are made manifest.* International

Association for Near-Death Studies. https://iands.org/ndes/nde-stories/iands-nde-accounts/1198-it-is-here-in-our-bodies-that-the-lessons-of-love-are-made-manifest.html

Anonymous. (2018, May 14). *Start all over in another lifetime or continue on with this one.* International Association for Near-Death Studies. https://iands.org/research/nde-research/nde-archives31/newest-accounts/1279-start-over-in-another-lifetime-or-continue-on-in-this-one.html

Anonymous. (2018, June 30). *From profound separateness to profound inclusiveness in an instant.* International Association for Near-Death Studies. https://iands.org/ndes/nde-stories/nde-like-accounts/1285-from-profound-separateness-to-profound-inclusiveness-in-an-instant.html

Anonymous. (2018, July 14). *Love was what everything was made of, came from, returned to.* International Association for Near-Death Studies. https://iands.org/research/nde-research/nde-archives31/newest-accounts/1289-love-was-what-everything-was-made-of-came-from-and-returned-to.html

Anonymous. (2019, June 10). *New mother feels loved beyond comprehension.* International Association for Near-Death Studies. https://iands.org/research/nde-research/nde-archives31/newest-accounts/1351-new-mother-feels-loved-beyond-comprehension.html

Anonymous. (2019, October 17). *Life review: Exchanging loving kindness with all.* International Association for Near-Death Studies. https://iands.org/research/nde-research/nde-archives31/newest-accounts/1382-life-review-exchanging-loving-kindness-with-all-2.html

Anonymous. (2020, April 19). *The physical world we experience is part of something vastly more complex.* International Association for Near-Death Studies. https://iands.org/research/nde-research/nde-archives31/newest-accounts/1454

-the-physical-world-we-experience-is-part-of-something
-vastly-more-complex.html

Anonymous. (2021, January 28). *Young woman sees life forms from other places and demon-like creatures.* International Association for Near-Death Studies. https://iands .org/research/nde-research/nde-archives31/newest-accounts/ 1503-young-woman-sees-life-forms-from-other-places-and -demon-like-creatures.html

Anonymous. (2021, July 8). *Vietnamese man in car crash accompanies his fiancée into light but returns alone.* International Association for Near-Death Studies. https://iands .org/research/nde-research/nde-archives31/newest-accounts/ 1548-vietnamese-man-in-car-crash-accompanies-fiance-into -light-but-returns-alone.html

Arnold, S., with Padorr, S. (2015). *37 seconds: Dying revealed heaven's help.* HarperCollins.

Arshan NDE. (1996). Near-Death Experience Research Foundation. https://www.nderf.org/Experiences/1arshan_nde.html

Arvind B NDE (n.d.). Near-Death Experience Research Foundation. https://www.nderf.org/Experiences/1arvind_b_nde .html

Brinkley, D., with Perry, P. (2008). *Saved by the light: The true story of a man who died twice and the profound revelations he received.* HarperOne.

Broome, K. (Producer). (2002). *The day I died: The mind, the brain, and near-death experiences* [Motion picture]. British Broadcasting Corporation. https://www.documentarytube .com/videos/the-day-i-died

Burton, C. (2002/2003). Counseling from a near-death perspective. *Vital Signs, 21*(1), 3–6, 14.

Bush, N. E. (2012). *Dancing past the dark: Distressing near-death experiences.* Parson's Porch Books.

Bush, N. E. (2016). *The Buddha in hell and other alarms: Distressing near-death experiences in perspective* (Kindle ed.). Author.

Bush, N. E. (2021). *Reckoning: Discoveries after a traumatic near-death experience.* Author.

Buyle, B. (n.d.). *Interview with Brigitte Buyle* [Motion picture]. Ponto3. https://www.youtube.com/watch?v=MOttjAkIFXs &t=178s

Caan S NDE. (n.d.). Near-Death Experience Research Foundation. https://www.nderf.org/Experiences/1caan_s_nde.html

Chen M NDE. (n.d.). Near-Death Experience Research Foundation. https://www.nderf.org/Experiences/1chen_m _nde.html

Chene, A. (n.d.). The near death experience of Nancy Rynes. https://www.youtube.com/watch?v=F-rp6bqfJWQ

Chenguan NDE. (n.d.). Near-Death Experience Research Foundation. https://www.nderf.org/Experiences/1chenguang_nde .html

Cicoria, T. (n.d.). *Dr. Tony Cicoria | Expressions | WSKG.* WSKG public media. https://www.youtube.com/watch?v= LYZ-rw9rJ90

Coppes, B. (2020). Heb je dan al liefde ervaren? [Have you already experienced love?] In R. Van Warven & R. Smit (Eds.), *Het Geheim van Elysion, 45 jaar studie naar Nabij-de-dood-Ervaringen over Bewustzijn in Liefde zonder Waarheen [The secret of Elysion, 45 years of study into near-death experiences about consciousness in love without whereto]* (pp. 143–145). Uitgeverij Van Warven.

Coppes, B. (2021/2022). Ieder mens is belangrijk (Everyone is important). *Terugkeer naar Levenslicht (Return to Life Light;* Journal of Netwerk NDE), 5(4), pp. 24–25.

Coppes, C. (2011). *Messages from the light.* Career Press.

Coppes, C. (2013). *The essence of religions.* SelectBooks.

Corcoran, D. K. (1996). *When ego dies: A compilation of near-death & mystical conversion experiences.* Emerald Ink.

Cox-Chapman, M. (1995). *The case for Heaven.* Putnam's Sons. (Quotes were taken from the Dutch edition and translated back to English; page numbers reference the Dutch edition).

Dale, L. (2008). *Crossing over & coming home: Twenty-one authors discuss the gay near-death experience as spiritual transformation.* Emerald Ink.

Dale, L., & Williams, K. (2022). *Crossing over and coming home 2: An analysis of LGTB and non-gay near-death experiences.* Balboa Press.

De Rijk, C. (2021). *Het kan ons allemaal gebeuren: Een hartstilstand en bijna dood ervaring veranderde mijn leven [It can happen to us all: A cardiac arrest and a near-death experience changed my life].* Boekscout.

Dye, E. (2023). *Lion magic.* www.lionmagic.com

Finch, R. (2019). *Conversations with my higher self.* Indie Blu(e).

Futrell, M. (2003). Not afraid of death—but not allowed to die. *Vital Signs, 22*(2), pp. 3 and 8–9.

Garrett, B. (n.d.) *NDE Michaela* [Motion picture]. https://www.youtube.com/watch?v=jTcHWz6UMZ8

Greyson, B., & Bush, N. E. (1992). Distressing near-death experiences. *Psychiatry: Interpersonal and Biological Processes, 55*(1), 95–110.

Halil T NDE. (n.d.). Near-Death Experience Research Foundation. https://www.nderf.org/Experiences/1halil_t_nde.html

Holden, J. M., Foster, R. D., & Kinsey, L. (2014). Spontaneous mediumship experiences: A neglected aftereffect of near-death experiences. *Journal of Near-Death Studies, 33*(2), 67–85. https://doi.org/10.17514/JNDS-2014-33-2-p67-85.

India physician NDE. (n.d.). Near-Death Experience Research Foundation. https://www.nderf.org/Experiences/1india_physician_nde.html

Jaswal, J. (n.d.) *Present!—Jan Jaswal's near-death experience* [Motion picture]. https://www.youtube.com/watch?v=eobvYMNPmRc

Javier, O. (n.d.). *Al Sullivan—Near death out of body experience* [Motion picture]. https://www.youtube.com/watch?v=u-91QXXsyEc

Jones, B. (2021). *Why are there monkeys? (And other questions for God)*. Luminaire Press.

Jones, B. (2023). *Written by Brooke Jones.* www.writtenbybrookejones.com

Jorgensen, R. (2007). *Awaking after life. A firsthand guide through death into the purpose of life.* Booksurge.

Kerry B NDEs. (n.d.). Near-Death Experience Research Foundation. https://www.nderf.org/Experiences/1kerry_b_ndes.html

Klein, T. (2006). *De kiem [The essence].* Uitgeverij Petiet.

Klein, T. (2008, March 4). Boven is dichterbij dan we denken [Above is closer by than we think]. *Mijn Geheim [My Secret], 32,* 48–54.

Krohn, E. G., & Kripal, J. J. (2018). *Changed in a flash: One woman's near-death experience and why a scholar thinks it empowers us all.* North Atlantic Books.

Lagae, G. (n.d.). *Interview with Geertrui Lagae* [Motion picture]. Ponto 3. https://www.youtube.com/watch?v=dCHbdVIBk7I&t=2s

Maltby, D. D. (2012). *While I was out . . . God came in: My near-death experience & soul altering journey.* Xlibris.

McDaniel, M. K. (2020). *Misfit in hell to heaven expat: Lessons from a dark near-death experience and how to avoid hell in the afterlife.* Franklin Rose.

Mendoza, M. A. (n.d.). *Deathbed visions of prisoners.* http://www8.webecs.com/PDF/AngolaPrisonStudy-MarilynA Mendoza.pdf

Mohammad Z NDE. (n.d.). Near-Death Experience Research Foundation. https://www.nderf.org/Experiences/1mohammad_z_nde.html

Moorjani, A. (2012). *Dying to be me: My journey from cancer, to near death, to true healing.* Hay House.

Moorjani, A. (n.d.). *Anita Moorjani's near death experience—Dying to live* [Motion picture]. International Association for Near-Death Studies. https://www.youtube.com/watch?v=tmT13Uuump0

Nancy R NDE. (n.d.). Near-Death Experience Research Foundation. https://www.nderf.org/Experiences/1nancy_r_ndes.html

Neal, M. C. (2012). *To heaven and back: A doctor's extraordinary account of her death, heaven, angels, and life again.* Waterbrook Press.

Neha S NDE. (n.d.). Near-Death Experience Research Foundation. https://www.nderf.org/Experiences/1neha_s_nde.html

Nightingale, J. (2006–2009). *Toward the light* [Talk radio show]. https://bbsradio.com/towardthelight

Petro, A. (2011). *Remembering the light through prosetry.* Outskirts Press.

Petro, A. (2014). *Alive in the light: Remembering eternity* (Kindle ed.). Outskirts Press.

Pols-Visser, T., & Oosterhof, M. (2010). *Verdwaald verlangen: Een zoektocht naar de hemel op aarde [Lost desire: A search for heaven on earth].* 248 Media.

Redant, M. (n.d.). *Interview with Marijke Redant* [Motion picture]. Ponto3. https://www.youtube.com/watch?v=8UPS3a hcHxY

Ritchie, G. G. (2004). *Return from tomorrow.* Fleming H. Revell. (Originally published 1978 by Chosen Books).

Rivas, T., Dirven, A. & Smit, R. (2023). *The self does not die: Verified paranormal phenomena from near-death experiences* (2nd ed.). International Association for Near-Death Studies.

Rogers, S. (1995). *Lessons from the light: Insights from a journey to the other side.* Warner Books.

Romona B NDE. (n.d.). Near-Death Experience Research Foundation. https://www.nderf.org/Experiences/1romona _b_nde.html

Rommer, B. R. (2000). *Blessing in disguise: Another side of the near-death experience.* Llewellyn.

Rynes, N. (2015). *Awakenings from the light: 12 life lessons from a near-death experience.* Create Space and Amazon .com in cooperation with Solace Press.

Sabom, M. B. (1998). *Light and death: One doctor's fascinating account of near-death experiences.* Zondervan.

Samieh NDE. (n.d.). Near-Death Experience Research Foundation. https://www.nderf.org/Experiences/1samieh_y_nde .html

Sawyer, T. (n.d.). *Tom Sawyer: His near death experience—Part 1.* https://www.youtube.com/watch?v=WH7lETcpjKo

Shalom G NDE. (n.d.). Near-Death Experience Research Foundation. https://www.nderf.org/Experiences/1shalom_g_nde.html

Sharp, K. C. (2003). *After the light: What I discovered on the other side of life that can change your world.* Authors Choice Press.

Sharp, K. C. (2007). The other shoe drops: Commentary on "Does Paranormal Perception Occur in NDEs?" *Journal of Near-Death Studies, 25*(4), 245–250. https://doi.org/10 .17514/JNDS-2007-25-4-p245-250.

Sneeden, Y. (n.d.). *Live heaven now.* www.liveheaven-now .com

Storm, H. (2005). *My descent into death: A second chance at life.* Doubleday.

Stout, Y. (n.d.). *A suicidal near-death experience and what it taught me about life* [Motion picture]. https://youtu.be/BMfjM6TrkV8.

Suicide NDE. (n.d.). Near-Death Experience Research Foundation. https://www.nderf.org/Experiences/1suicide_nde.html

Suleman, A. (2004). *A Passage to Eternity.* Amethyst.

Taylor, S. M. (2001). *Near-death experiences: Discovering and living in unity* [Unpublished doctoral dissertation]. University of St. Thomas.

Taylor, S. (n.d.). *Shared death experience—Scott Taylor—four people meet the light together* [Motion picture]. www.youtube.com/watch?v=M3YeSCgHug8.

Thornton, L. (2014). *Through heaven's gate and back: A spiritual journey of healing and what it taught me about love, life, and forgiveness.* Lulu.

Thornton, R. (2021). *Remembering the light: How dying saved my life.* Gentle Beam.

van Lommel, P., van Wees, R., Meyers, V., & Elfferich, I. (2001). Near-death experience in survivors of cardiac arrest: A prospective study in the Netherlands., *Lancet, 358* (9298), 2039–2045. https://doi.org/10.1016/S0140-6736(01)07100-8

van Lommel, P. (2011). *Consciousness beyond life: The science of the near-death experience.* HarperCollins.

Vengroff, C. L. (2012). *My ever after chronicles.* Balboa Press.

Xue-Mei C NDE. (n.d.). Near-Death Experience Research Foundation. https://www.nderf.org/Experiences/1xue_mei_c_nde.html

Yazmine S NDE. (n.d.). Near-Death Experience Research Foundation. https://www.nderf.org/Experiences/1yazmine_s_nde.html

Index

About the Author

Robert Christophor Coppes holds a PhD in economics and worked for many years at the University of Groningen in The Netherlands and in the banking industry. Bob was in a commercial position with a French bank and later in a supervisory role at the Dutch Central Bank—equivalent to the U.S. Federal Reserve. He has recently retired to write and lecture.

His conviction that near-death experiences are true spiritual experiences dates back to 1979 when he read Raymond Moody's 1975 book, *Life After Life*. In 2006, Bob wrote a book that was published only in the Netherlands in which he compared the essences of NDEs with those of five world religions. This book was translated into English and published in the US in 2013 as *The Essence of Religions*. However, his first book in the US, *Messages From the Light*, was published in 2011. It was also translated into Dutch and German. The message he got from his many interviews with NDErs is that the 2008 financial crisis was the consequence of people's focus on *short-term self-interest*. It would be more beneficial if we changed our focus towards *long-term "our-interest."*

Also, please visit his websites (www.bobcoppes.com or www.nde -unconditionallove.com) and visit his YouTube channel with the QR code provided for short introductions to some of the subjects in this book:

Made in the USA
Middletown, DE
25 March 2024

52067892R00144